The Bowhunting Life

Forty Years Hunting with the Bow & Arrow

by

Ralph Blackwelder

A Blackwelder Books Publication

www.BlackwelderBooks.com

Book Cover Photo: Ralph and the "Riding Stable Buck" - see Chapter #2

Contact Ralph at:

BlackwelderBooks@gmail.com

www.BlackwelderBooks.com

ISBN: 978-0-9835-7080-6

Blackwelder
Books.com

Key to Good Reads

www.BlackwelderBooks.com

"*The real archer when he goes afield enters a land of subtle delight. The dew glistens on the leaves, the thrush sings in the bush, the soft wind blows, and all nature welcomes him as she has the hunter since the world began. With the bow in his hand, his arrows softly rustling in the quiver, a horn at his back, and a hound at his heels, what more can a man want in life?*"

~ Saxton Pope (1875-1926) ~

"Hunting with the Bow and Arrow"

A Word from the Author about Bowhunting and Safety

- Always wear and use a safety strap/belt when hunting or practicing from a tree stand. Especially, when climbing up the tree, coming down, and when stepping onto the stand.

- Don't climb a tree with your bow & arrow; pull them up after you're settled safely in your tree stand.

- Never shoot at anything that you can't clearly see and identify.

- Keep broadheads pointed away from you at all times.

- Always ensure no one is down range when target shooting. Everyone should be standing somewhere behind you as you shoot.

- Obey all hunting laws and regulations.

"When a hunter is in a tree stand with high moral values and with the proper hunting ethics and richer for the experience, that hunter is 20 feet closer to God."

~ Fred Bear (1902-1988) ~

"The Deer Hunter's Prayer"
~ Dale Sunderlin ~

Heavenly father, to you I pray,
A majestic deer may come my way.
Let my aim be straight and true,
this my Lord, I pray to you.

A swift clean kill is what I ask,
Take his spirit swift and fast.
For his last breath should not be,
One of pain or agony.

Let his soul,
Come to Thee,
To roam your heavens,
Wild and free.

DEDICATION

~ This book is dedicated to the late Kelly Hillman ~

T hank you, Kelly for being such an important part of my life and for taking the time to take a young boy hunting. We discovered bowhunting together, before it was popular. I was lucky to be there on the mountain with you when you shot your first deer with a recurve bow. I don't know who was more amazed? It was like you did it for me, to encourage me, and to show me that I could do it too, and to inspire me to keep trying.

You were with me on the mountain in the snow when I shot my first buck with a recurve. I am still living by the lessons you taught me: never give up looking for a wounded deer, and always treat animals with respect and dignity.

The love of the outdoors is a precious gift that really belongs only to those who live a certain kind of life. Thank you for giving me that gift when I was in my teens. I have been blessed to be able to enjoy the outdoors all of my life.

You are always there with me during the hunt. When you passed, the hunting world lost a true master huntsman and outdoorsman. I lost the best hunting companion anyone could ever have.

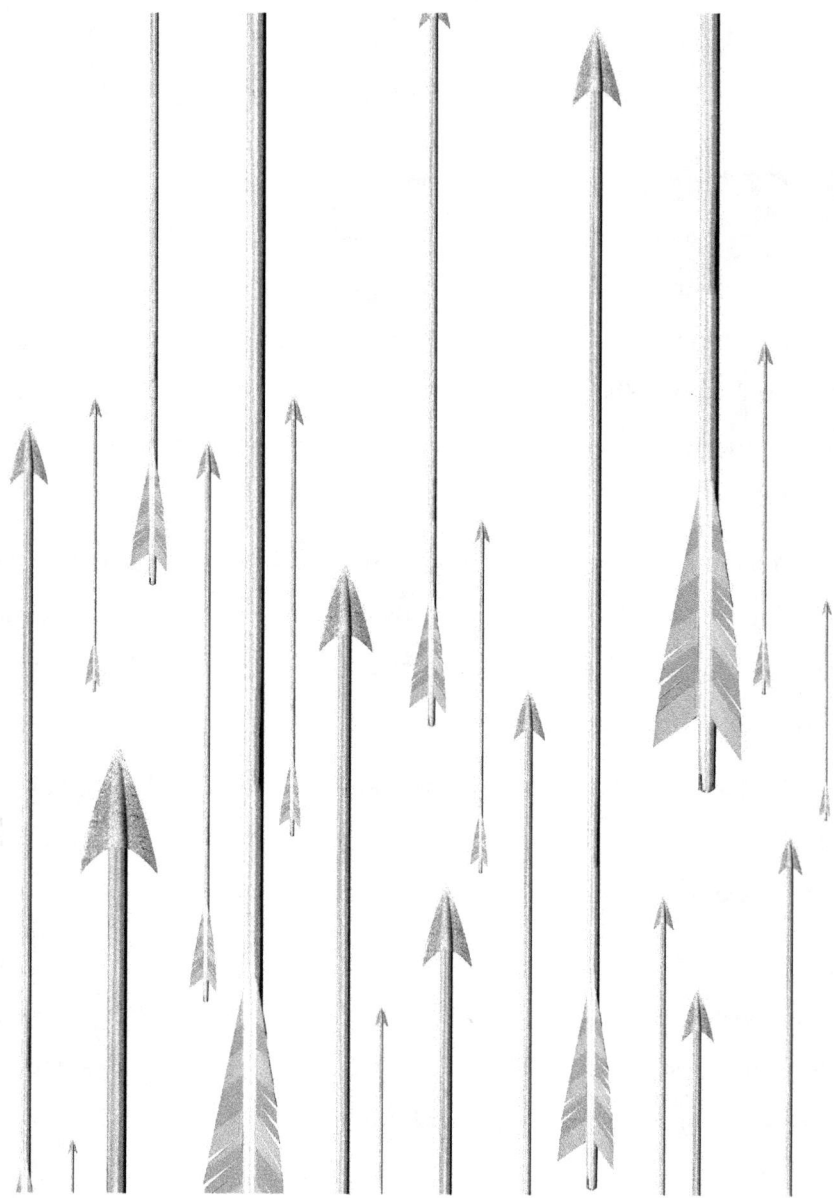

TABLE OF CONTENTS

My wife Lisa with the results of a perfect morning
we spent together in the turkey woods

ACKNOWLEDGMENTS

My mother and father always supported and encouraged my love of the outdoors and bowhunting. Mom had to deal with all the creatures that I'd bring home from the woods: snakes, possums, bullfrogs, turtles, and anything else unable to get away from me. I kept squirrel hides in my room, and taught myself how to tan a hide in a bedroom closet. My father would take me to wildlife and nature speaking events. He always watched my favorite outdoor TV shows with me. Dad also introduced me to our next-door neighbor, Kelly Hillman, who took me hunting and changed my life forever.

My two boys, Josh and Clayton, both roamed the woods with me as kids and have always had to share me with Mother Nature. *Thank you guys!*

Over the years, I've had the pleasure of sharing the woods with many great hunting partners. The outdoor experience lives forever when memories are made with your hunting friends. I want to acknowledge a few really special hunting buddies: Jim (Tim) Timmerman and Dan Mumpower.

My wife and soul mate, Lisa, has always encouraged, appreciated, and shared my love of hunting and the outdoors. We made a memory of a lifetime when she bagged a boss gobbler on our first turkey hunt together. She has raised two boys (really three, if you count me), gotten in a tree stand with me, and learned to shoot a longbow.

I LOVE YOU – SWEETY!
~Finders Keepers~

He's not a monster, but what a life-changing trophy!

This is my first deer with a longbow. I used a Martin 80# longbow and homemade cedar arrows. This buck started my fascination and love of the longbow and traditional archery. As you can see, I was a rookie as far as scent control goes. I had not yet learned the importance of wearing rubber boots.

1

MY LOVE FOR BOWHUNTING
~the early years~

I inherited my love and fascination with the outdoors from my grandfather, a South Carolina mill worker who loved frog gigging, gambling, and whiskey - not necessarily in that order. When he wasn't down at the river pitching pennies, fishing, or turtle hunting, he was wading through a midnight swamp, frog hunting side-by-side with the water moccasins. As a school kid, I would spend my summer break in South Carolina with my grandparents, where my grandfather would take me along on his adventures to the river and swamp. Those wonderful outdoor experiences with him planted the seed, and built the foundation for the bowhunting life I would lead.

In my early teens, I became quite an outdoors enthusiast. My father worked for DuPont in Delaware, and I grew up on land surrounded by a game preserve that was full of deer and other wildlife. And because our house was also less than a mile from a trout stream, I spent every waking minute daydreaming about my next opportunity to wade the stream with my fly rod. I was constantly trying to hook the ole granddaddy of a brown trout. At other times, after getting permission to fish a local pond, I would strap my rod and reels to my bike and peddle the five miles to school so that I could stop and fish the pond once school was out. I don't think anyone took my fishing very seriously until I came home one day with a five-pound bass strapped to my bike. My mother took pictures, and submitted them to "Sports Afield" magazine. I was shocked and surprised when an award arrived in the mail, and my name was published in the magazine as having caught the record largemouth bass for 1967 in Delaware. Generally, when I wasn't fishing the streams or pond, I was roaming the nearby forest in search of deer to stalk. My favorite TV shows at the time were "Mutual of Omaha's Wild Kingdom" and "The American Sportsman."

My interest in archery began as a teenager back in the early sixties. Around the age of fifteen, archery and bowhunting came into my life. I saw a Howard Hill movie clip and watched Fred Bear on the "The American Sportsman", show hunting Grizzly Bear with his recurve bow. That was it! I knew that I had witnessed the ultimate hunting challenge, and have been an avid archer and bowhunter ever since.

My early years in archery were spent shooting three or four times a week after school at Jim Glass Archery, in Kennett Square, PA, one of the first, fully indoors and automated archery ranges in the United States. I joined an archery league, and spent a lot of time getting very good at hitting a two inch dot at twenty yards. During this time, my bowhunting exploits included shooting at countless stumps, rabbits, and pheasants. A 'Bear Archery' recurve bow was my pride and joy.

When Tom Jennings put the first compound bow on the market, I was very skeptical and didn't think it would amount to much. However, like most archers of that time, as the new archery gear and aluminum arrows grew in popularity, I replaced my recurve with a Jennings compound bow. Compound bows dominated the archery market for many years, and it appeared that recurves and longbows were forever a thing of the past.

My compound bow shooting lasted until the early 1980s. I was heavily into the southeastern 3D tournament shooting circuit, and won many first place ribbons and trophies in the bare-bow division - a competition which involved shooting with fingers and no bow sight. I never used a sight or release aid while shooting with my first compound bow.

My love of hunting was stronger than ever. During the 1980s, my military career placed me at Fort Gordon, Georgia, just outside the city of Augusta. I was born in Clinton, South Carolina, and the South has always been in my blood. Being stationed in Georgia was like coming home. The deer and turkey hunting on Fort Gordon and the nearby wildlife management areas were what dreams are made of. During the week, I would shoot over 100 arrows a day with my compound, then spend the weekends hunting and shooting 3d tournaments all over Georgia and South Carolina. Little by little, though, I became dissatisfied with the compound bow. I was shooting robin hoods (one arrow into the tail end of another) and, eventually, the enjoyment of archery was replaced by a lot of work and frustration. I needed to find a new challenge. Archery was not enjoyable for me anymore!

In 1983, I read the Howard Hill book, "Hunting the Hard Way", and bought my first longbow - an economical, 80# straight limb Martin. Almost overnight, I was transformed back to my recurve days and my interest in archery sky-rocketed. Within a short period of time, I was extremely accurate with my longbow and cedar arrows. Walking through the woods with a longbow and back quiver full of hand-made arrows was all the medicine I needed to energize my love of archery. I practiced at close range and didn't hunt with my longbow until I was extremely confident shooting at fifteen yards. I think I shot at every stump on Fort Gordon that first year of practice. By the fall of 1984, I had perfected crafting my own cedar arrows, and was ready to take my stick and string and get back to deer hunting. The season was almost half over before I got a chance to use my new weapon on an archery-only wildlife refuge hunt. I stayed on-stand all morning; then, around noon a small eight-point came up the trail towards me. As he walked behind a tall Georgia pine, I prepared for the shot. He stepped out from behind the tree and, as his front leg moved forward, I drew, picked a spot, and released, all in one fluid motion. I don't know any other way to explain it other than to say, "I rode the arrow to the deer" and instantly knew I had made a great shot. I found the deer less than thirty yards away. The Howard Hill broadhead, that I learned to sharpen with a file, had done its job.

Up to that day, I had probably harvested well over fifty deer with a bow and arrow, but that hunt is the one that will forever be etched in my memory. Archery, for me, changed on that special day in 1984! The buck was not as big as others I had taken, but I had him mounted, nonetheless. I often admire him, now, in my study and relive that hunt. The longbow and traditional archery have been a passion of mine ever since. I found my way back to my roots with archery and have never looked back.

Chapter 1 - My Love for Bowhunting

Over the years since that first longbow buck harvest, my immersion in the art of traditional archery grew. I began to craft all my arrows, and a desire to build my own custom longbow led me to read everything I could on bow building. The bowyer side of archery began for me in the mid-1980s, when I built my first longbow while stationed in Korea as a service member. I used hand tools from the base wood working shop, and my service footlocker in my barrack's room became a crude bow building form. It took me over six months of the one year tour to complete the bow - a straight limbed, great shooting longbow that I'm very proud of today. By the way, the Koreans couldn't get over how I held my own using my homemade longbow and arrows on a pheasant hunt on an island off the mainland of Korea. I brought down as many pheasants as the gun hunters, and I know I had more fun.

I am presently retired from the Army and teach computer technology classes for the local community college, here, in Augusta, Georgia. My bow building developed immensely over the years, and I can say without bragging that my bows are equal in craftsmanship, and perform as well, as anyone's. Along the way, I've refined and perfected procedures that make building a quality longbow both easy and very enjoyable. Maybe, someday soon, I'll write a book explaining my longbow building techniques.

I'll be sixty one this year and have developed severe arthritis from the many years of pulling heavy bows. Archery has come full circle for me, and I'm now shooting a modern compound bow. I struggled for a few years with trying to balance how much I could shoot my longbow before the pain in the shoulder, wrist, and fingers stopped me from being able to hunt at all. Going to the woods has always been what's really important to me. I'll miss carrying the light-weight longbow that, for years, had been such a natural part of my hunting experience. I'm accepting the compound bow with excitement and as a new challenge.

This book shares with you a few short stories of my bowhunting life, along with deer and turkey hunting tips to increase your odds of becoming a successful bowhunter. Enjoy!

Making a longbow by hand in my garage

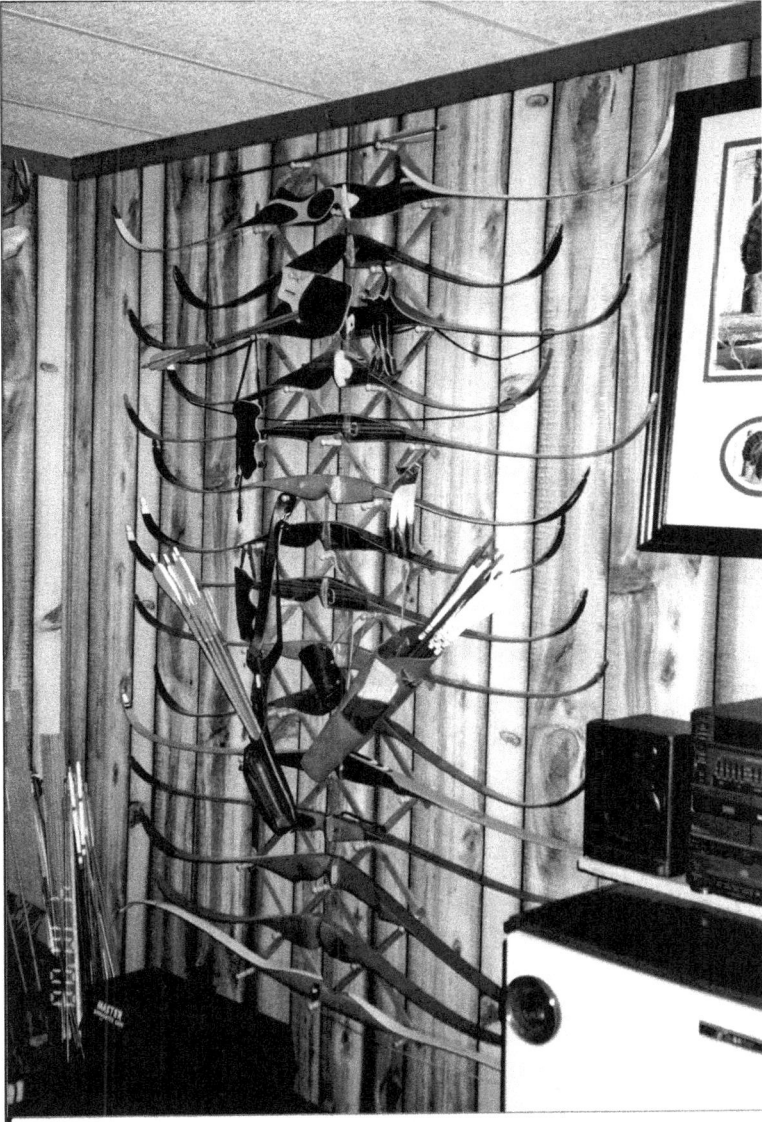

My recurve collection

A few of my custom built longbows.

I started crafting my own custom longbows in the 1980's using a few hand tools in my garage.

"It is said that every ten years or so the story needs to be told again to refresh the memory of those who lived it and bring the story to those who are new to the sport"

~ Glenn St. Charles – Billets To Bows ~

I used my "Connect-the-Dot" scrape method to tag this mega buck. I hunted the "Riding Stable Buck" for three years before being able to bring it to this moment. Notice the rubber boots for scent control.

2

CONNECT-THE-DOT SCRAPE HUNTING
~Making special scent trails to interconnect scrapes~

T he misty ground fog that had been making visibility difficult finally lifted. The sudden sunlight was a welcome sight. Two days of rain had dampened the forest and I could barely hear the squirrels scampering through the leaves behind me. From the nearby swamp came the unmistakable sound of turkeys flying off their roosts. Their fly-down told me they had been waiting for the rain to stop before coming down to feed. I knew the deer would be moving now, too.

I was in my portable stand 20 feet up a Georgia pine. I was wet to the bone and a pine tree knot was poking into my back. My leg, hip and back ached from hours of sitting motionless in a tree stand. Yet I was filled with a sense of heightened anticipation and awareness. A slight, cool breeze fanned my face. Everything was perfect.

My stand was smack in the middle of a lure-connected triangle of mock scrapes I'd made an hour before light. I hung this particular stand up the previous afternoon during a rainstorm. Rain, I've found, offers the perfect opportunity to scout and hang portable stands without leaving a lot of human scent. A hundred yards or so behind me an oak ridge held trees heavy with mast. Several deer trails led from the swampy bedding area to the ridge – and the falling acorns, which lured hungry whitetails like kids to candy. I had a good view of the Georgia swamp bottom for at least 30 yards on every side of my stand. The only thing missing were the deer.

A flicker of white alerted me to the small buck easing through a thicket just in front of me. He cautiously approached the mock scrape on my right with his neck outstretched, nostrils flared. It was close to 10:00 and this was the first deer I'd seen all morning. My hunch that the deer would be moving once the rain stopped looked to be panning out.

Many years ago I started reading about mock scrapes and how to use them to consistently tag big bucks. Since using mock scrapes – along with rattling and grunting – my bowhunting success has at least doubled. And there is one special method I have developed that has been especially effective. I call it my "connect-the-dots" method because it interconnects scrapes by special scent trails. It has refined my scrape hunting by creating a situation which consistently maneuvers bucks into my confident shooting range of 20 yards or less.

First, I'll describe the hunting area and equipment. Next, I'll explain how "connect-the-dots" scrape hunting works.

I am fortunate to be able to hunt on Fort Gordon, Georgia, a U.S. Army military installation located on the outskirts of Augusta. Fort Gordon has an abundance of whitetail deer and turkey and I consider it a bowhunter's paradise. The woods consist mainly of pines or oaks and the terrain varies from swamps and hardwood bottoms to hills and ridges. Hunting on the Fort is open to I.D. Card-holding military or retirees, their dependents and guests. There are areas designated for bowhunting only. Since I rarely gun hunt, most of my hunting is done in these bowhunting areas.

Chapter 2 – Connect-the-Dot Scrape Hunting

I was shooting cedar arrows from a Heritage Archery longbow or a longbow I've made myself. I really appreciate the lightweight simplicity and beauty of the longbow. But with my longbow I must limit my shots at whitetails to 20 yards or less. Wearing full camouflage and knee-high rubber boots is essential. They're as important to me as keeping my broadheads razor sharp. I've had good success using fox urine on my boots as a cover scent, along with keeping clean and washing my clothes in baking soda.

Most of my deer hunting is done from tree stands. Personally, I favor portable, strap-on stands; they function nicely on virtually any tree without damaging the trunk. I invented a tree climbing system called "Fas-steps" back in the late 1980's, and have used them for years with outstanding success. They are quick, featherweight, easy to use and don't damage the tree. Fas-steps were the first of a kind, tree climbing system, and originally sold as a new product by the Warren and Sweat Manufacturing Company. Over the years, "Fas-steps" have been replaced by many different types of tree climbing systems.

My method of scrape hunting employs mock or real scrapes connected by a dotted trail of doe-in-heat lure. After I've pinpointed a particular buck's feeding, bedding and breeding areas, I place my portable stand in a "high confidence" area. When I'm hunting mature bucks, finding such areas is often done on a gut feeling generated from experience and scouting data.

Remember, older bucks can be very unpredictable. Finding and interpreting deer travel patterns, rub lines, scrape lines and staging areas for the bucks in your own hunting area are musts if you plan to be successful. You need to get the big picture of the day-to-day core area activities of the deer you're hunting. Year-round scouting will increase your deer hunting wisdom tremendously. The trick is to learn all you can about the area you're hunting without disturbing the resident mature bucks. I scout as if I'm still-hunting. Slow movements, rubber boots, cover scent and full camouflage are necessary for effectively scouting with the least disturbance to an area. Shut your eyes and mentally walk through your hunting area. Your scouting is coming together when you can envision a buck's feeding, bedding and travel hot spots. Once you've done your homework, you will recognize "high confidence" areas and know where to place your stand. The gut feeling you'll get will be well deserved and should pay off.

After hanging my stand, I then make a number of mock scrapes around my stand. Each is connected to another by a dotted line of doe-in-heat lure. Each scrape is approximately 15 to 20 yards from my stand and 30 to 40 yards from each other. The number of "connect-the-dots" scrapes I make depends on the availability and location of the classic overhanging licking branches. The idea is to entice the buck to one of the mock scrapes and have a lot of shooting options. I can arrow him while he's at the scrape, if a good shot is presented, or I may have a better shot as he walks over to check a scent-connected mock scrape.

The dotted lure trail between the scrapes will always bring him directly past my tree stand. The connected scrapes are also placed close enough to each other for the buck to see another scrape while standing on or in the vicinity of one. This visual connection has proven to be invaluable and is often the key in persuading the buck to walk between the scrapes for the perfect shot opportunity. To ensure that the buck can see the scrape, I generally make fairly large scrapes under licking branches. If you can see them easily from 30 yards, they're big enough. I paw out the mock scrape with a stick while wearing rubber gloves, then pour doe-in-heat lure in each scrape.

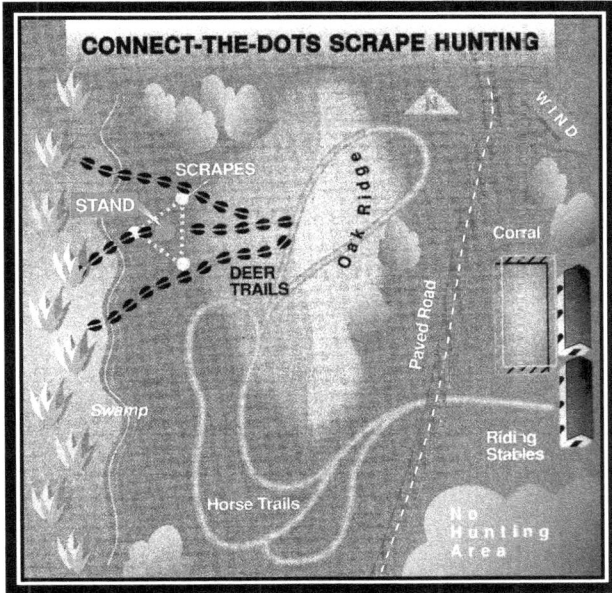

Diagram of "Connect-the-Dot" scrape hunting

I knew that the buck approaching my stand wasn't the deer I wanted. A huge buck I called the "Riding Stable Buck" was my goal – and this was his home turf. I gave him his nickname because this little-hunted area is flanked by a horse riding stable. Horseback riders often travel the logging trails and back roads throughout this area.

It was November 10 and the rut was well under way. I had climbed into my stand – and endured hours of discomfort – with high hopes that once the rain stopped the "Riding Stable Buck" would come my way. I figured he should want to freshen scrapes while looking for does in heat. And I had faith that my "connect-the-dots" scrapes would get his attention if he passed my way.

Meanwhile, I enjoyed watching the small buck's reaction to my mock scrapes. As he came closer, I counted six small, evenly matched points. He would be a fine trophy someday but he wasn't what I was looking for. He nosed around the right hand scrape for only a minute or two, then after noticing the connected mock scrape on my left, started straight for it. Earlier, I'd created a doe-in-heat lure trail between the two scrapes and now the small buck followed it like a bloodhound. I held my breath, hoping he wouldn't scent me and snort an alarm, as he went past my stand only 15 yards in front of me. He sniffed at the left hand scrape and thrashed the overhanging limb with his small rack. About five minutes passed before the buck did an about face and went back the way he came. Again, he walked within 15 yards of me. My confidence level in this scrape hunting strategy was soaring. If only the "Riding Stable Buck" would come.

I was determined to stay on the stand at least through lunch. Patience and staying in a stand is something I'm used to. At the time, my vocation as a U.S. Army Master Sergeant developed in me the unlimited patience and discipline needed to remain motionless for long periods.

Later, as I was getting a snack from my pocket to stop my growling stomach. I heard something advancing from behind and to my left. Knowing there are a lot of squirrels in the area and their nut-gathering on the oak ridge had been an ongoing operation all morning, I suspected that this was the same fox squirrel I'd seen earlier. But as the sound got louder, I recognized the unmistakable sound of a buck grunting softly. Moving as slowly as possible, I stood and braced for a shot. When the buck materialized at the left hand scrape, I instantly recognized him. It was the "Riding Stable Buck."

I had been after this particular buck for three long years. There had been many times when I came close to outsmarting him – but something invariably went wrong. More than once he circled my stand from a safe distance as if somehow using his sense of smell to calculate exactly what tree I was in. He would then stare at me from 30 to 40 yards. How he knew I wouldn't shoot from that distance, I'll never know. And he would always win the stare-down no matter how hard I tried not to move. As soon as he was satisfied he had sufficiently frustrated me, he would vanish.

It became an annual contest. I truly believed he would have been disappointed if I'd given up the chase. The more perplexing he became to hunt, and the more mistakes I made, the more determined I became. Believe me; I spent more time sitting in trees hunting this buck than I spent at home. I'd come to know the area where he lived as well as I know my own living room. This had not been just a seasonal thing either. I'd hunted his sheds and sign during the off-season and prowled his domain all year long. Now he was just below me.

Exceptional for this area of Georgia, with nine long points and an extremely wide antler spread, he was a buck to behold. Now, as he turned his head to lick and smell the overhanging branch at the left scrape, I raised my 64-pound longbow and picked a spot. Experience told me to wait for a better angle. I paused. He saw the other connected scrape and started toward it. My "connect-the-dots" strategy was working. As he walked past I could see his long tines, gray face and rut-swollen neck. My heart was pounding. My knees were shaking. I tried not to look at his rack. Regardless, buck fever had grabbed me. I couldn't believe it was him. The "Riding Stable Buck" had never been this close to me before.

One of the "Riding Stable Buck's" rubs

Chapter 2 – Connect-the-Dot Scrape Hunting

I practice close shots regularly and was very confident of my shooting skills. If my stomach didn't growl or he didn't scent me, I'd make a good shot. But I had to start my mental pre-shot countdown to calm myself. When he passed me at 15 yards with his nose to the lure trail, I came to full draw, anchored and released in one fluid motion. I instantly knew my shot was true.

Years of instinctive shooting has programmed my brain to picture the flight of the arrow even before release. This arrow couldn't have come off the bow better. The Snuffer-tipped cedar arrow entered the vitals behind the buck's shoulder. Instantly he staggered, almost falling, then ran back the way he came. I saw my fletching protruding just behind his shoulder.

I've taken a lot of deer over my lifetime as a bowhunter. From the angle of the arrow, I knew it was a lethal hit. Regardless, I was trembling and sat down on the stand. I'd finally fooled the "Riding Stable Buck" and couldn't get over how incredibly well my "connect-the-dots" scrape hunting had worked.

Thirty minutes later I was tracking him, following a solid blood trail which quickly led to where he had piled up. And even though the hunt went perfectly, the shot was unforgettable and the deer magnificent, I felt somewhat saddened that our yearly chess game was over. I'll always look back on the seasons I spent hunting the "Riding Stable Buck" and savor the memories. He will be hard to top.

Author's Notes

At the time of this hunt, this was the third buck in two years that I'd tagged using the "connect-the-dots" scrape hunting tactic. Although I've tried a lot of different tactics in an effort to get deer in close for pointblank shots, nothing has worked as well as connecting the scrapes. It's a strategy that works for me and I'm convinced it will work on bucks in any whitetail area. So if there is a buck that's been outsmarting you, give "connect-the-dots" scrape hunting a try during this year's rut. You might be pleasantly surprised at the results. You can bet I'll be connecting scrapes to outfox another trophy whitetail.

The Riding Stable Buck

Of course I'm in shock! My spring gobbler - the hard way.

3

SPRING TURKEYS THE HARD WAY

I wasn't prepared for the case of the jitters I got as the mature gobbler came into view. I knew I was well camouflaged, but I still didn't think I could get my longbow into action fast enough when the right moment came. I'd been working this bird with a slate call and every cluck I put out was answered with a strong gobble.

I could see him through the brush pile I was hidden behind as he came up the deer trail out of the swamp bottom. He was in full strut and I could tell he was a mature bird by the long, even tail feathers and how his beard almost dragged the ground. I guessed his weight at between 22 and 24 pounds.

The strength and volume of his clucks was having a nerve-shattering effect on my ability to get the wooden shaft on its way. I didn't dare even blink. When I judged him to be at 10 yards I knew I had to make my move or risk having a very excited gobbler try and make me his mating partner....

That 1986 turkey season on Fort Gordon turned out to be a rewarding experience that made me a turkey hunter forever. I'd wanted to try my hand at turkey hunting for many years but never seemed to know just how to get started. When I'd finally get hooked up with a local turkey diehard willing to show me what I'd been missing, the season would be over.

I was in the Army and stationed in Korea in 1985, when I met Dan Mumpower, who loves to hunt turkeys... and anything else, for that matter. Since we couldn't hunt turkeys in Korea, we spent plenty of time talking about it and I read everything I could get my hands on about hunting them.

By January 1986, we were both stationed at Fort Gordon and we started some pretty heavy preseason scouting. Since I'd been stationed there before, I was very familiar with the area and found out that a lot of my old deer hunting stomping grounds were ideal locations for ole Tom.

Prior to 1986, I'd been involved in archery for about 20 years and enjoyed bowhunting so much that I didn't even own a gun. In 1983, I decided to switch from my compound to a more traditional longbow. I started making my own wooden arrows and during the 1984 deer season tagged a nice eight-point buck with my 80-pound longbow. I've been hooked on the longbow since and was determined to tag a Georgia spring turkey the same way. I'd be using a new 66-inch Robertson Stykbow, 70 pounds at 28 inches, with wooden arrows tipped with Bear Razorheads.

Dan and I found that there was a very good population of turkeys in the area and had very good success calling birds in during our preseason scouting. Fort Gordon is a hunting paradise of hardwood swamps, ridges of scrub oak, pine thickets and nesting fields – all prime turkey habitat. We had no trouble locating turkeys roosting in along the swamp bottoms where they could fly down into the fields and feed on the grasshoppers and crickets, or they would work the ridges scratching for bugs and acorns. Finding the fresh tracks of a mature bird is important in building confidence that you're not hunting hard where there aren't any birds; we found a lot of fresh jake and tom tracks throughout the areas we decided to hunt.

Chapter 3 – Spring Turkeys the Hard Way

Dan is a seasoned turkey hunter who was overjoyed to have an eager student to hunt with, even if he was a little pessimistic about our chances of collecting a bird with a bow. I was not able to get a reliable yelp with the diaphragm call no matter how hard I tried, but I kept practicing so that by the following year I would have the confidence needed to reliably produce good yelps. My calling ability was limited in the beginning to some pretty questionable calls on one of Dan's old slate calls, so it was decided that the majority of our hunting would consist of Dan calling for me while I waited in ambush behind a camo net. I practiced my shooting daily before the March 28 opener and got pretty good at hitting the paper bird at unknown distances.

Opening morning the temperature was much cooler than normal and we couldn't get a bird interested in Dan's yelps. For bowhunting turkeys by yourself, the diaphragm mouth call is the way to go. It's difficult to put the box or slate down to pick up the bow when the turkey is within seeing distance and I'm a firm believer that ole Tom can see your hair growing at 100 yards.

The next few days found Dan and me up at 3:00 a.m. so we could be on the birds at first light and into work by 9:00 a.m. We worked a few birds but just couldn't put it all together to nail one. The fourth day of the season was a classic example of how our feathered friends were outsmarting us. We heard a bird gobble as we steeped from the car and, knowing that he was a long way off, decided to double time so that we could set up on him before he got with the hens.

My favorite turkey set up when using a longbow

It's important to be in top physical condition when turkey hunting. Running up ridges through scrub oak, combined with getting up at 3:00 every morning, can really take it out of you if you're not in peak condition. If the gobbler is already with hens when you get to him, you've lost a lot of the battle before you even start. To a gobbler, a real hen in the bush is worth two decoys any day.

After a lengthy run, we set up on him by placing our hen decoy in between Dan and me, but in such a way that the bird would walk past me to get to the decoy. This would allow me a shot with the bird facing away, his attention on the decoy and Dan's clucks.

Chapter 3 – Spring Turkeys the Hard Way

It's imperative to keep safety in mind when setting up a two-man operation so that the caller is safe from flying arrows. We also learned that it's best to set up with the rising sun on your back, especially if you're like Dan and me and wear glasses. A turkey knows that there is nothing in his area of operation that reflects the sun like your glasses would. Complete head-to-toe camo is also a must.

I was sitting on a stool behind a camo net when Dan started yelping. On about his third yelp the old tom double-gobbled from in close, indicating his intention to come in. He came along the ridge at a trot and it looked like everything was finally coming together. He was a mature bird that would go about 24 pounds. In full strut he worked his way to the decoy. I had an arrow nocked, just waiting for him to walk past my blind for a shot. As the wary ole Tom got right in front of me, he tensed; he knew I didn't belong there. He gave the alarm putt, dropped low to the ground, and started running back up the ridge at full speed. The instant he alarmed, I rose up from behind the camo net and fired off an arrow that barely missed, going a little high over the gobbler's back. Background camo, such as a bush or tree, might have helped me blend into the surroundings better; a turkey at three feet can see through any net that a hunter can see through.

On the evening of our fifth hunting day I had to hunt alone because Dan had a commitment at work. And although my confidence in calling a turkey myself wasn't real strong, I wanted to try. I was hunting in an area where a fire from the previous summer had left a lot of new vegetation on the edge of a swamp bottom. It had been a deer hotspot for me in the past.

Position yourself so that you can get off a quick
shot when gobbler hunting with a bow.

Chapter 3 – Spring Turkeys the Hard Way

It wasn't long before I heard his gobble. I moved in as close as I could and still be out of sight and sound. I didn't have the decoy or the camo blind with me, so I chose a brush pile to set up in. Surprisingly, I produced some very nice clucks! The tom gobbled back after every one and, by the loudness of his gobble, I could tell that he was on his way.

At 10 yards it was difficult to put the slate in my pocket and prepare to shoot without alarming the bird, but he cooperated by turning his back to me and spreading his tail feathers – which hid his head long enough for me to draw, anchor and shoot. The arrow hit where I aimed without passing through. He ran about 30 yards back into the swamp before piling up.

I was so excited that I stood there and shook for several minutes before going over to admire my beautiful trophy. He weighed in at 22 pounds and his beard measured 10 inches. There has never been a prouder moment for me than when I carried that bird home over my shoulder. I knew from that moment on that I'd become a diehard turkey hunter.

Thanks to Dan, I was able to combine his expert teachings, hours of shooting practice and a healthy dose of beginner's luck to successfully bag a spring turkey… the hard way.

It don't get no better!! I'm just sayin....

*"Any old Indian can kill a deer with a bow, but it takes
a Chief to kill a turkey with a bow"*

~ Ben Rogers Lee ~

Here I am with a home-made longbow and cedar arrows on a Spring turkey hunt. Position yourself up in the brush and along the side of a tree if possible. Notice the full head-to-toe camouflage.

4

TIPS FOR BOWHUNTING GOBBLERS

Preparation:

- Wear full camouflage. Face net (especially, if you are like me, and wear glasses), camo gloves, etc.. Head-to-toe camo is a must if you plan to get within ten to fifteen yards or closer to a gobbler.

- Make sure your equipment is as camouflaged as possible. Anything shining and the turkey will see you from way off.

- Practice patience and sitting still. Use a stool or kneeling, but you must be able to stay absolutely motionless for long periods. Patience is the number one skill you need to master and take with you every time you go to the woods.

- Bring a hen decoy. I'll share with you how to place the decoy in the "setup" section later in the chapter.

- Bring a couple of different types of calls, so that you can sound like a small flock of hens. I have a favorite box call, which was given to me by a hunting buddy, Dan Mumpower. That call has lured many gobblers to an early grave. I also like the slate.

- Practice calling and know how to make as many types of hen calls as possible. Don't get too hung up on this; I have called in many gobblers with a simple yelp on the box. It's not about how much, or the quality of the call. The key is to know when to call and when to stop calling; use the bird's natural curiosity and need to breed to your advantage.

- Bring bug spray. You will need it! A little toilet paper in your pocket never hurts either.

- Be cautious of crows and squirrels. A crow, once they locate you, will give away your position to every living thing in the woods. Squirrels barking at you can also alert game to your presence. Work at becoming a master woodsman as well as hunter, and know how your intrusion into the woods effects all of the wildlife. *This holds true for deer hunting as well.*

The Setup:

- I like to get behind a portable camouflage net blind if possible. If the gobbler is close or coming in quickly, and you don't have time to get behind a blind, then get on your knees and up into a bush or up against the side of a tree where you are hidden, but can still shoot your bow.

- Place the decoy about fifteen yards in front of you and facing you. You want the hen decoy with its back to the gobbler as the gobbler is coming in. He won't be able to stand it when she won't look at him and he will circle to get in front of her. This will give you a close shot as he comes around between you and the decoy.

- Double-team on gobblers; a favorite technique of mine is to get a hunting buddy to call for me. Have the caller setup so that the gobbler is pulled past you, giving you a close shot. Be careful not to shoot in the direction of the caller.

- ***Never*** setup facing into the sun. If possible, you want to be in the shadows to help you hide, and you don't want the sun in your eyes or reflecting off of any of your equipment. With the sun in your face, you won't be able to see the gobbler, but he will certainly see you.

Calling:

- I'm a huge believer in calling to get his attention, then shut up and concentrate on how you are going to get the shot off when he comes in.

- Space your calling out and don't call just because you have not heard or seen anything in the last ten minutes. If you have scouted the area and know the birds are roosting close by, then have confidence that they have heard your call and are coming. BE PATIENT!

- Always imagine that the gobbler is just over the rise and coming. Coax him in over the rise with feeding calls. Scratch in the leaves a little to sound like a hen scratching as she looks for acorns. Then get your bow and arrow ready and be still and patient.

- If the gobbler gets hung up and is just not going to come any closer, try backing up fifty yards and set up again. This sounds to the gobbler like the hen is moving away. Often, this will help bring him your way. Frequently, running away from the sound of a gobbler before setting up is more productive than moving in too close and running him off. Especially if you're like me and have poor hearing.

I love it when a plan comes together ....

I had a great morning in the turkey woods…. two gobblers with my longbow and cedar arrows.

Equipment & Shooting:

- ***Practice, Practice, Practice*** at close range and shooting quickly. If you are not hidden behind or in a blind, the gobbler will more than likely see you as soon as you move to draw. You will only have seconds to get the arrow off.

- GET USED TO MISSES. I have shot a gobbler through the head, so I am not a poor shot. But I have loss count of how many arrows I have shot over a gobbler's back. Bowhunting turkey is one of the most challenging hunts you can attempt and you should expect to miss a few. Some of my most memorable hunts are the ones where the gobbler spots me at the last minute and I missed. But the look on that old boss gobbler's face when he looked over and saw me behind the blind with the bow ready will stay with me forever – he gave the alarm putt, then dropped low to the ground as I was coming up to shoot over the blind, and off he went like a road runner with my arrow just skimming his back. What great fun. What a great hunt, and what a memory.

- Practice shooting from your knees, and in the blind that you will use. An excellent practice for turkey hunting can be roaming through the woods during the off season, stump shooting from a kneeling position, and while crouched in a bush.

- Keep your equipment as simple as possible – there's less to go wrong at a critical moment. I like to turkey hunt with the same gear I use to hunt deer. If you are shooting a compound bow, try lowering the draw weight for turkey. You'll be able to hold at full draw longer, which could come in handy, and you don't need a heavy weight bow to kill a turkey.

The Shot:

- It's my experience that the best shot on a gobbler is right through the tail feathers and into the center of their back as they are strutting and facing away from you. They are less likely to see the movement of you drawing and shooting. Their head will be hidden by their tail feathers and hopefully looking away from you at the decoy.

- Don't shoot at the whole bird. Just like deer hunting, *pick-a-spot.*

Know your hunting area:

- Learn everything you can about the turkey in your hunting area. Know what they are eating, where they roost, and where the strutting zones are.

- It is especially important with turkey hunting that you know who else is hunting the area. If others are hunting within hearing distance of you, it's best that the gobbler does not gobble, but comes to you quietly. His gobble will attract other hunters and more than likely they will bust up the hunt.

Safety:

- Always be aware that there could be other hunters coming to your call thinking you are hens with a gobbler close by, especially if a bird is gobbling. These hunters might have guns. You are totally camouflaged and not easy to spot in the woods. If you see another hunter, shout as loud as you can. Make sure they know you are in the area. Then leave and go hunt somewhere else. You will not kill a boss gobbler with unknown numbers of hunters running all over the woods, and it makes for a dangerous situation.

- Once you harvest your bird, drape an orange hunter safety vest around the bird before throwing your trophy over your shoulder and heading out to show him off.

- Always understand and obey all hunting laws and regulations.

This boss gobbler hung up on me, and I had to move away from him numerous times to finally get him in close enough for my home-made Osage longbow.

You got the boss gobbler - if you can hang him on a tree limb by his spurs

My 2012 Spring Gobbler – 22 lbs

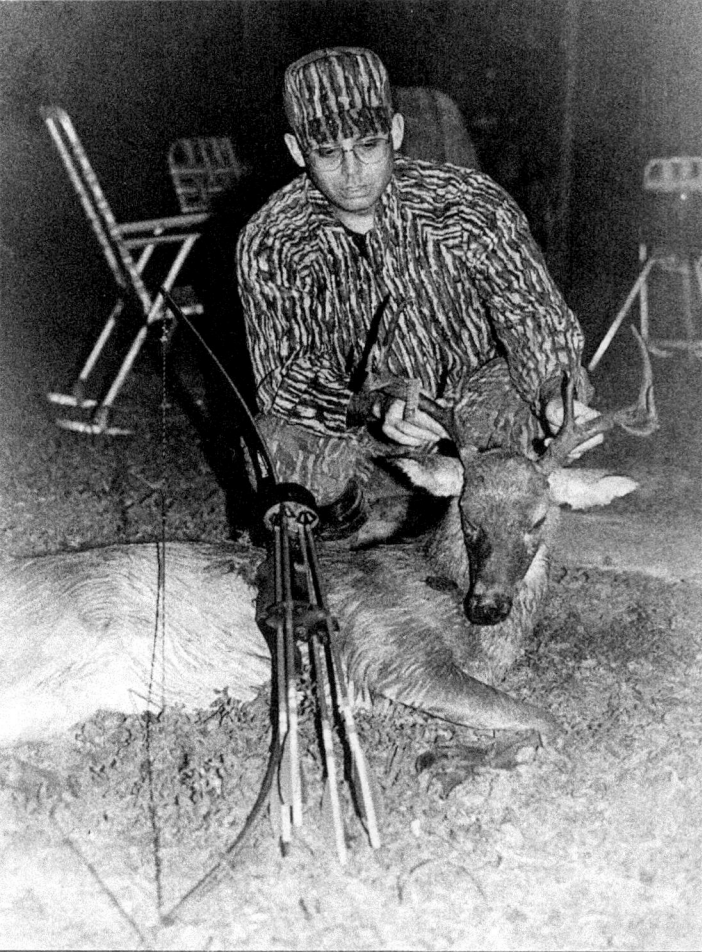

A nice longbow swamp buck becomes a victim of my
"Hanging Socks" funneling method.

5

HANG YOUR STOCKING

I told myself not to look at the antlers as the buck worked his way slowly toward me through the pine thicket. Failing this, I mentally went through my checklist of things to do in order to be ready for the shot. The eight-pointer stepped into the small clearing 15 yards from my stand. *Bingo!* This is what it's all about. My 70-pound longbow and the Snuffer tipped cedar arrow performed well; the buck went only 40 yards before piling up. I got my buck because I maneuvered him into an ambush situation that put the odds of getting the shot in my favor.

I know that there are bowhunters that tag deer every year with 30- and 40-yard shots. I'm not one of these people. Years ago, I accepted the fact that in order to consistently put meat on the table with a bow, I needed to be as close as possible to the deer without being too close to shoot. I bet you're thinking. *How can a deer be too close to shoot?* Try getting off an arrow at a deer that is within five yards of your stand and you're 15 to 20 feet up. It's very difficult and not the ideal situation. No matter what the distance, shot presentation must be perfect if we are to kill cleanly.

Hunting with a distance limitation on the shot has always been what makes bowhunting for deer the rewarding experience that it is. This involves getting the deer to stand just where you want him. For me that place is 10 to 20 yards away, at a good angle. Over the years I have tried every method that I could come up with plus anything that was suggested to me for consistently getting close shots at deer. I've tried rattling, calling and mock scraping, all with some success.

An extremely productive method I have used to get deer where I want them is what I call the "stocking" method. Now, stocking your own deer in an area like you would stock fish in your pond would be an excellent way to put deer where you want them, and I agree with you. However, this is not how it works. I call it the stocking method because I use the socks we wear on our feet to funnel deer into the area that will give me the shot I want.

Bowhunters are continually trying to hide their scent from deer. I've found that human scent is very nearly impossible to cover completely. About all you can do is mask your scent in hopes that the deer will not identify you as a threat. I like to use human scent as a method of funneling deer to me and to indirectly mask my own scent. That is, I use human-scented socks to saturate the outskirts of a large area that I know is home to the buck that I'm hunting. I set out these socks to form a funnel. The base of the funnel will be a 40-yard wide area where I use commercial masking scents to hide my own human scent. In the middle of this area is where I place my stand. This gives me a 20-yard shot on either side of my stand to cover the entire base of the funnel. I've found that the extremely strong human scent of the socks will have a definite masking effect on the scent present in the stand area. This works much the same way that the aroma from the tasty hamburger you are eating can be lost among the stronger odor of the other burgers cooking on the grill.

I stumbled across this method many years ago during a hunt in an area heavily populated with deer. From my stand I watched deer walk down a small ridge 50 yards in front of me and work their way around me much too far for me to shoot with confidence. By lunch-time I had watched 12 deer follow the same route without one offering me a shot. There weren't any good stand locations on the route the deer were traveling, and I didn't want to scent up the whole area by roaming around trying to locate a stand site. I decided to try to maneuver the deer to me by using parts of my clothing. I went out to the trail they were using and by hanging my T-shirt, socks and sweatshirt on tree branches, formed a funnel which turned the deer in my direction. It worked! By 2:00 p.m. I had passed up shots at smaller does and made a 10-yard shot to take a 140-pound doe.

To ensure that you fully understand the method of my madness, look at Figure 1. This is a drawing of a point on a large lake in Georgia. It is a bowhunting-only area which I have hunted for the past five years with a lot of success. I usually park my car where the logging road starts at the main dirt access road shown on the bottom right of the drawing. I like to be set up and in my stand at least an hour before light. It's important to be in place before the other hunters who hunt along the main access road hit the woods. The area between the main access road and stand site B is a large bedding area with thick patches of honeysuckle and young pine.

I'll enter the woods from the logging road at site A and angle my way to stand site B. During pre-season scouting I've marked the way with glow-in-the-dark tacks, so finding site B in the dark is not a problem. When hunting with my buddies, site A would be where one of us would set up a stand. As I work my way slowly into site B, I hang or tie socks, which I have kept at the bottom of my clothes hamper for maximum human scent saturation. I hang them close to the ground, one about every 40 yards.

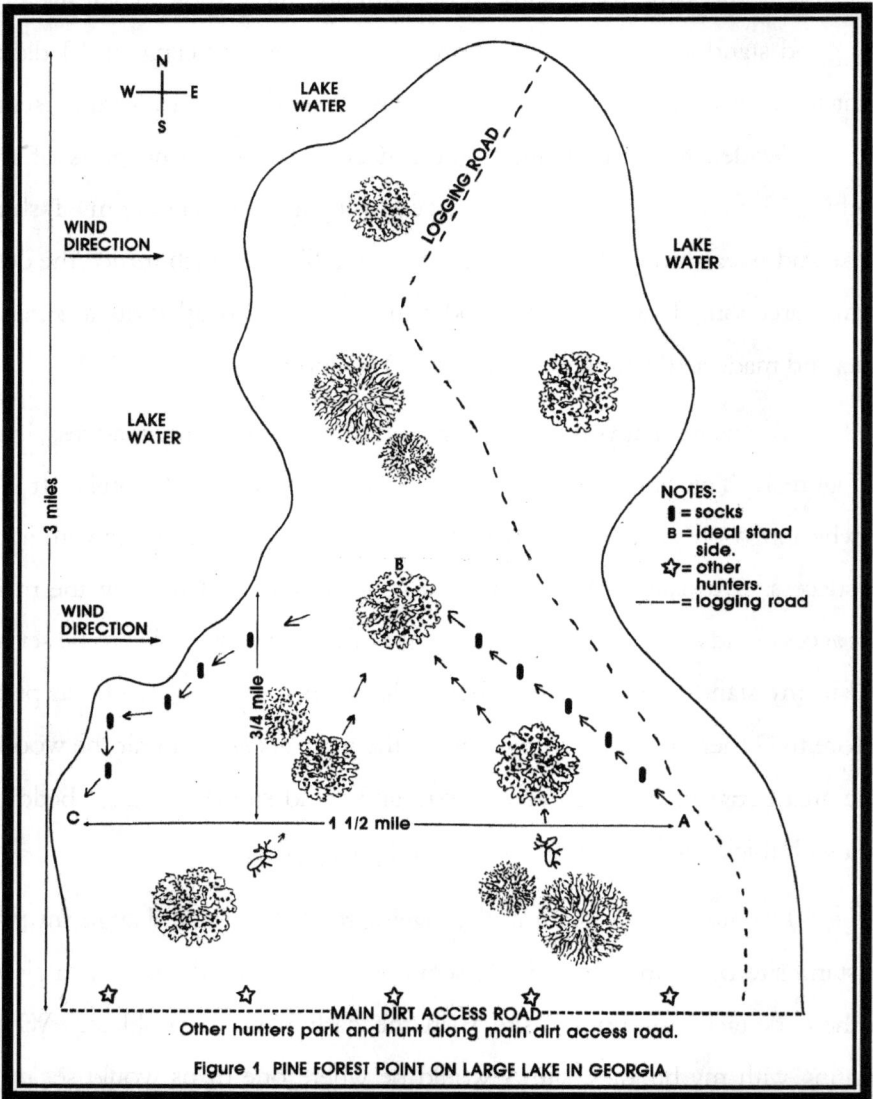

Figure 1 PINE FOREST POINT ON LARGE LAKE IN GEORGIA

Figure 2

I usually set my trail markers where I want my socks set out so I can find these places easily. This also aids in finding the socks on the way out of the woods late in the evening. I don't leave anything in the woods; old socks are litter, as are trail markers, and I don't want it said that bowhunters litter.

About 40 yards out from site B, I put the last sock on that leg of the funnel. This spot is marked with two trail marker tacks. From this spot on into site B, I use a masking scent. You can't use too much! It's important that you convince the deer that humans have not been in this portion of the woods. I'll also use a buck lure (doe urine) around the stand, but not closer than 10 yards. I don't want him in too close!

After arriving at site B, I leave my stand and bow and then proceed to site C. This trail is also marked. Here again, if I'm hunting with a buddy, one of us continues to site C and the other sets up at site B. I repeat the same process of hanging out the socks on my way to site C, but the first one is at least 40 yards out from site B. If hunting by myself I return to site B after reaching site C. Socks hung up along the route to site C make up the other leg of the funnel.

You can see now from looking at the drawing that the lines representing the hanging socks form the sides of a funnel which feeds site B. With a little help from proper wind direction and other hunters moving around, the deer, trying to stay away from the scented socks, will work their way into bow range of the hunter at site B.

It is very important when using this method to stay on your stand as long as you can. Stay all day, if possible. In most cases the hunters in the area will go to their cars for coffee and sandwiches when they get tired of sitting. Their movements will stir deer, and anytime deer are moving in the area they'll be avoiding those socks! In the case of the area in my drawing, the lake and the logging road also form natural obstacles for deer. Hunters at sites A and C should be ready for deer who are trying to sneak back out and around the funnel. I have found that these hunters often see as many deer as the bowman on site B.

I realize this is an unorthodox way of deer hunting, but believe me, it works! I've taken numerous deer from stand site B, including two eight-pointers I knew were using the area. This method has also been very successful for me in swamps. Obviously, you aren't restricted to using socks. Any rag will do. I like socks because they are easily hung or tied to branches, and my wife won't let me put rags in our clothes hamper. Everyone at one time or another lost socks to the sock fairy. Ask your wife how many times she has washed clothes and come up with an odd sock. Instead of throwing out the odd sock, save them for this fall's deer hunt. You only need about 10, and you can use them year after year. Dump them in the bottom of your clothes hamper a few days before opening day and you're all set.

Always keep the following in mind when setting up a sock ambush in your favorite hunting area:

- If other hunters use the area, learn their movements and try to use them to direct the deer to your location.

- Always set up so as to use natural deer obstacles – water, roads, fences, etc. – to direct deer to your location.

- Be aware of wind direction. My experience has been that a cross-breeze is best, but not mandatory.

- Get there early and stay late.

Before you decide that this method won't work for you, give it a try. Pull out a map of our hunting area, and plan out the funnel ambush on the map. Believe that if you seriously try this method you will "sock it to bucks" in your area.

A buck I took with my recurve using turkey yelps to bring
him in close. Notice the knee high rubber boots. I'm
somewhat of a fanatic when it comes to scent control, and
have almost always worn solid rubber boots when deer
hunting.

6

YELP & CLUCK TO GET YOUR BUCK

It looked like it was going to be one of those mornings when you felt deer movement in your bones, but before you knew it, the morning had passed by with the only movement being your knees knocking from the cold. It was a beautiful, cold, clear, fall day that I couldn't help but enjoy no matter how unproductive the hunting.

I was trying very hard to memorize the loud, rhythmic yelps that were coming from the swamp only a couple hundred yards from my stand. I love to bowhunt spring turkeys and I'm always trying to improve my calling techniques. What better instructor than the wild hen. Here in the Central Savannah River Area of Georgia, just outside of Augusta, there is no fall turkey season. I've found that it's an excellent time to practice calling, and mimicking the hen cluck and yelp without the worry of making a mistake which normally cost you a gobbler in the spring. I make it a point to carry a turkey call with me when deer hunting. You never know when you're going to get an opportunity to practice, and yelping is an excellent way of signaling your hunting buddy that you're approaching his stand site.

Just as I was about to use my box call and let go with another practice yelp, I saw movement just on the outside of an oak clearing. Putting away the turkey call as quietly as possible, I got my longbow into position for a shot. The buck stepped into view at about forty yards. Much too far for what I feel would be a confident shot, but close enough for me to tell he was a very nice eight pointer. He didn't seem alarmed at all, and was feeding very heavily on the acorns that covered the ground. What sounded at first like more deer feeding into the clearing turned out to be four turkey hens. The buck didn't seem to notice as the hens fed to within a couple of feet of him and they all seemed to be competing for acorns. I've watched a lot of deer feed in the past, but I'd never seen a buck so relaxed and seemingly unconcerned about any possible threat. Normally they'll stop feeding every few seconds to lick their nose and test the wind. I've found that feeding deer will rely heavily on their nose, and my theory is that the crunching noise of eating, especially acorns, inhibits their hearing. This deer wasn't acting as he should, and at the time I didn't know why.

The buck and turkeys were feeding farther away from me, and it was looking very much like I wasn't going to get a shot. Normally I'll use a tube type grunt call to get a buck's attention and try to draw him in, but I had left my grunt call at home. They were out of sight now, but I could still hear them munching acorns, and was desperately trying to come up with a way to bring him in my direction.

Then it hit me! If I could bring the hens my way, maybe the buck would follow. The more I thought about it, the more logical it seemed. I've hunted turkeys long enough to know, you can't sneak up on them. What safer place for a buck to feed than with a bunch of wary hens. He was letting the turkeys set up his defense perimeter for him, knowing that if a predator entered the area they would set off the alarm. Plus, at this point, I had nothing to lose by trying out a theory.

I started making light clucking sounds, followed by a very low yelp that was so realistic I found myself wishing my hunting partner was there to hear how my calling had improved since last spring. I really wasn't surprised when the hens stepped back in the oak clearing and headed my way. I was only about twelve feet up in a pine. Anyone who has hunted wild turkeys knows about the importance of camouflage. I was totally camouflaged except for my Robertson Stykbow which has a pine straw color. As I tried to calm myself and concentrate on not making any movement that would end what seemed to be a plan that just might work, the buck seemed to appear from nowhere. I needed the hens to feed past me without being alarmed if my plan to get the buck to follow them into shooting range was to work.

We've got a long archery season here in Georgia, which has given me a fairly good opportunity to try deer-yelping. I've yelped in over fifteen deer to within a few yards of my stand during the first four months since I discovered this method. My hunting partners have had even better success.

The majority of my deer hunting is done on Fort Gordon, just outside of Augusta, Georgia. There is a very good population of wild turkey and deer. The terrain is primarily swamp and creek bottoms with scrub oak and pine hillsides. The deer and turkey both feed on the overabundance of acorns, and it's usually a good bet that when a lot of deer sign is found in an area, there will also be a lot of turkey sign.

I've found that the amount of camouflage usually needed for deer hunting is not sufficient when trying to yelp them in close. If turkeys are present when deer-yelping and they come to the call with the deer, concealment is at least twice as difficult due to the outstanding eyesight of the wild turkey. A drawback to deer-yelping is that the deer tend to look for the source of the yelping. It's not uncommon for deer to walk in on a hunter very quickly before the hunter even realizes the deer is in the area. It's been my experience that if yelping is done from a tree stand, the deer will approach looking up. This calls for extra alertness, no noticeable movement, and complete head-to-toe camouflage. Getting higher up in the tree than I normally would has also kept a few deer from spotting me. When deer-yelping I place my tree stand around twenty feet up. I've tried using ground blinds when deer-yelping and while succeeding in getting deer to investigate the yelps and clucks, I've been unsuccessful in getting a shot from a ground blind. This is not to say that it won't work. Using tree stands when deer-yelping has worked so well that I haven't spent much time using ground blinds. It's human nature to stick with what works!

The diaphragm call is the most convenient type of call when deer-yelping, especially when bowhunting. It leaves the hands free to hold the bow and allows you to continue soft clucks when the deer is close enough to see any movement that might be made using other types of calls. Basically, the same call you use during the turkey hunting season will work when deer-yelping.

It's very important to realize that the idea is not to bring in any turkeys with your yelping, but to suggest to any deer in the area that turkeys are feeding where you are, and that it's both a good feeding spot and a safe place to be. If yelping does bring in turkeys, it makes it much more difficult to get off a shot at a deer. It doesn't take much to spook a turkey, and it's very difficult to watch approaching deer while also keeping an eye on a flock of feeding hens and gobblers. If deer do approach while feeding with a flock of turkeys, don't shoot until you are one hundred percent sure you will not injure any turkeys. Here in Georgia, the penalties for hunting wild turkey out of season are extremely stiff, and should be. We have come a long way in restoring the wild turkey throughout the country, and should do everything possible to see that this progress continues.

This brings me back to the approaching buck at the beginning of the story. The turkeys were clucking softly as they scratched their way past my stand. I just knew they would hear my heartbeat, and spook at any moment, but lady luck seemed to be with me as they moved over to feed under an oak ten yards behind me. I kept my eyes on a spot just behind the buck's shoulder, while staying aware of the turkey's location behind me. The next sequence of events convinced me that using a turkey call to yelp in deer was a sound discovery. The buck started moving away from me at the moment I was preparing to draw and shoot. All I could do was watch as he fed away from me. I could hear the turkeys scratching ten yards behind me and was afraid of yelping for fear of bringing their attention to me at such close range. It was looking like a no win situation that was going nowhere fast. I took a deep breath and let out the most beautiful yelp/cluck combination you could imagine. The buck stopped and looked in my direction, and I swear he looked right at me. I willed myself to become part of the tree. Up to this point I had worked very hard for this buck. My nerves were a wreck, and I wanted this deer very badly. As I mentally begged him to "come on", "come on", one of the hens answered my yelp and he trotted the thirty yards to my stand. If you've ever had a buck at the base of your tree, you have a pretty good idea of what I was trying to deal with. He was too close for a good shot. To make things worse, the hens were moving over to feed with him directly under me.

I will always believe that the doe that stepped into the clearing was attracted to the oaks by the sound of my yelping. She started in the direction of the oak I was in, but as soon as she saw the buck, turned and trotted back to the swamp. This rejection seemed to confuse the buck and he moved slightly in the direction of the doe, which put him broadside at fifteen yards. I don't remember ever taking my eyes of the spot on his side I had picked to shoot at, and quickly had a snuffer tipped cedar shaft on its way. The arrow hit with a solid whack, and the eight-pointer was in the swamp in only two or three leaps. I'd forgotten about the hens, and as they spooked from all the commotion, it startled me so bad I dropped the arrow I had prepared to nock for any possible second shot.

After giving my nerves a few minutes to calm down, I got down from the stand, and went over to begin the job of digging my arrow out of the pine tree. Yes, I know you've heard it before, but there really was an unseen twig that deflected my arrow into the pine. As I dug around the broadhead to free it from the tree, I had time to reflect on what had happened. It would have been tremendous to have tagged the buck, but that seemed unimportant compared to the excitement of the past thirty minutes, not to mention how excited I was about discovering deer-yelping.

If you deer hunt in an area inhabited by wild turkey, carry your turkey call on your next deer hunt. You'll be able to practice your turkey calling during those moments when you feel you just can't sit still any longer, and you'll probably find it a thrilling challenge to "yelp and cluck to get your buck".

Author's Notes

In researching to insure that use of a turkey call during deer season, and out of turkey season, was legal, I contacted the Georgia Department of Natural Resources, Law Enforcement Section in Thompson, Georgia. They stated that there was no hunting regulation that would make my deer-yelping discovery in any way illegal.

I have never been more proud as a bowhunter, than when I harvested this mature doe. Using my homemade solid cherry self-bow and cedar arrows, I was able to stalk to within fifteen yards before making the shot from the ground.

7

CRITIQUING THE HUNT

You're in the tree stand before light, just as you have been an average of three days a week for the past 45 days of the deer season. You were up late last night and didn't hear the alarm go off this morning. But your wife did and turned it off, without kicking you out of bed. The dog barking next door, finally woke you an hour before light. The fact that you hadn't seen any deer in the last week of hunting, convinced you to just stay in bed and continue the dream of the monster buck that made the huge scrape in the swamp bottom. The dog next door wouldn't shut up, and as thoughts of bucks with rocking chair racks, turned to thoughts of all the work you needed to do around the house, you decided to get up and go hunting. In your rush to beat first light, you didn't shower and still smell of last night's Old Spice.

The wind is blowing your scent all over, but your enthusiasm isn't dampened because you're 15 feet up in the closest tree to the largest scrape you've ever seen. No one could call you a rookie if they considered the number of hours you have spent in your stand, over the past three years as a bowhunter. Sure, you've had shots on numerous occasions, but something always seemed to go wrong. You deserve a medal for your dedication and persistence, and as always, you feel this will be the morning you tag your first deer with a bow.

The squirrels playing under your tree startle you awake, and while trying to focus on the surrounding forest, you spot a buck feeding on acorns only 15 yards in front of your stand. He's a six pointer that would look very nice over the mantle in your den. Not wanting to blow the chance for a shot, you stand up, draw, and shoot, all seemingly in one motion. The arrow passes just beneath the deer's belly and buries itself in the forest floor. You've stopped breathing altogether now, as the deer takes two steps in your direction and continues to feed. You can't believe that he's still there, but calm yourself enough to realize you're about to release the second shot, without an arrow on the string. Pulling an arrow from your bow quiver, all too noisily, you nock it, draw, and shoot. The deer falls down. Climbing and falling from the stand, you run up to the deer, which has been hit in the spine, and end any suffering with a heart shot.

How familiar this must be for many of us. To a lot of bowhunters, except for the bragging, back slapping, and celebrating, this would be the end of the season. The story is a common one. It's obvious that mistakes were made, but the deer was tagged, due to a combination of persistence, luck, and the cooperation of a deer bent on committing suicide. Although we, as a whole, need these suicidal deer, every bowhunter should work towards improving hunting skills so that mistakes like missing easy shots and continually hunting in the wrong place at the wrong time, become things of the past. Not taking advantage of lessons-learned ultimately ends in a dramatically lowered degree of confidence. It's becomes more and more difficult to tag deer with a bow when you depend solely on luck, and the deer's cooperation. Every year, deer become a little wiser, and seem to adapt quicker to man's hunting methods.

Chapter 7 – Critiquing the Hunt

There is an area I have hunted for years, which is only open to bowhunters. A majority of the hunters use treestands, and tend to leave the woods before lunch, to return to their stand in the late afternoon. Over the last few years, I have watched an increasing number of deer come by my stand, looking up in the trees. The deer in the area also tend to increase their movements around noon. These deer have adapted to the treestand method of hunting, over a relatively short period of time. I plan to try a ground blind and stay on stand through the noon hours, in the hope of capitalizing on the survival instincts which cause deer behavior to change, as they become wiser to the hunting methods used in their area.

Let's hunt next year's deer today, by admitting to mistakes made on our last hunt. Sit back and evaluate how to improve your hunting so that you lessen the degree of luck needed to tag your next deer. No matter how much you feel that you're a good hunter, and are following all the basic rules of good hunting, there are always ways to improve. In order to learn from our mistakes, we must first admit to making mistakes, and then we can identify and correct them.

I've developed a bowhunter's critique worksheet that over the years has helped me to thoroughly analyze each deer hunt. Webster defines "critique" as "a careful analysis of work." If you're like me, you work harder at bowhunting than anything else, because it's what you enjoy most. By helping me identify my shortcomings, and increasing my knowledge of game behavior, the critique sheet has increased my confidence as a bowhunter, tremendously.

I no longer feel that I need to depend on a suicidal deer's cooperation in order to put meat on the table with a bow. I've learned to be honest with myself about mistakes, and by listing them on the critique sheet; they are imprinted deeper in my mind.

I've found that because my critique sheet has a place to record wind direction, in relation to feeding and bedding areas, that I pay much closer attention to wind direction when placing my stand. Critiquing your hunt on paper, or using a word processor, also gives you a fantastic historical record of all your hunting adventures. Spending evenings before opening-day pouring over previous years' critique sheets is as important to me as the time I spend in the field doing my pre-season scouting. I fill out a critique worksheet after every hunt, and being honest about mistakes, put in as much detail as needed. It usually takes only 15-20 minutes to fill out, which for me, has proven to be time extremely well spent. It has consistently paid off with meat on the table.

The critique worksheet is divided into three sections. I call these sections: data, mistakes made, and sketch. Using the example illustration, let's look at each section so that you'll have a better idea of the types of information that can be entered on the worksheet.

First, look at the "data" section along the right side of the worksheet. This is not the most important section of the worksheet, but does contain information that is good to have. You'll notice first that this was an evening hunt on October 8, 1984, and that my hunting partner was Randy Riedlinger. We got set up in our stands at approximately 3:30 p.m. and left our stands at 6:10 p.m., for a total of 2 hours and 45 minutes.

My bowhunter's Critique Worksheet. It would be easy to use a word processor or a note taking app on a tablet computer.

For me, this is a good way to document the time spent hunting. The weather was clear and cool, with a high temperature for the day of 64 degrees, and a wind velocity of 3 mph. I get the day's detailed weather information from either the cable TV weather station or a telephone call-in weather information service. I use the "deer/turkey sighted block" to tell me how many, what sex, and when during the day, game was seen. I circled deer in the example to indicate that only deer were sighted. Circled turkey would indicate only turkey were sighted, and if my partner or myself had seen both deer and turkey, I would circle both. I indicate nothing sighted by a line drawn through both. When you're preparing for turkey season, it's fantastic to be able to quickly glance through the critique worksheets and have at your fingertips, details of areas where turkeys were sighted while deer hunting. It also works just as well when you're turkey hunting and sight deer. If you're like me and have trouble remembering your own birthday, let alone where and when you saw the most game two years ago, this becomes an invaluable tool.

Before looking at the next section of the example, I want to mention that many other bits of information can go on the worksheet. For instance, if you are a two season hunter, and hunt with both gun and bow, you might want to enter the type of equipment used. This could be entered under the date of the hunt, or most anywhere on the worksheet.

Next we'll discuss the section I call "mistakes made." This section, along with the sketch, makes up the most important part of the critique worksheet. I've numbered this section 1 through 10, but I never seem to be able to fit what I want to say in the small space beside each number, so I usually disregard the numbers, as you can see in the example. I write down everything I honestly feel I did wrong on a particular hunt, to include criticisms and comments from a hunter partner. I will also frequently jot down notes that I feel will help me better hunt an area in the future, even though it might not refer to any mistake made. For example: if an animal was tagged, I would definitely note somewhere in this section the approximate age, weight, and stomach contents of the animal. Entries are limited only to your honesty, imagination, interest, and what you personally feel is necessary in making you a smarter and more confident bowhunter.

The last section entails drawing a rough sketch of the hunting area to the level of detail you desire. If possible, I orientate the sketch in relation to the pre-dawn compass headings at the bottom of the page. This becomes essential when orientating the sketch to a topographical map of the same area. If I'm very familiar with a location from numerous hunts, then the sketch is not very detailed. If it's a new area, I put in as much detail as space will allow. I always have a pencil and paper in my hunting shirt with which to sketch and take notes while in the woods. I can't rely on my memory for necessary landmarks, once I've gotten home and decide to fill out the critique worksheet. In the example, I'm fairly familiar with the hunting area, so I limited the sketch to stand sites, deer trails, and main feeding and bedding locations. It's very important to keep in mind that it might be years before you hunt the same location again. What's obvious to you as you draw the sketch will in all likelihood be gone from your memory three or four years later. So putting in too much detail is always better than not enough. As shown in the example, I draw an arrow in the wind direction square so that it points in the direction that the wind was blowing. If the wind direction changes, I write in "the mistakes made" section, the wind direction changes as best I can. When changing stand sites while hunting, I'll number them on the sketch, with number 1 being the first stand site of the day. I'll also put the time I moved, on the sketch. Quite often this corresponds to notes I've made on changing wind direction.

The layout and design of the critique worksheet is not as important as how you use it. If the one I developed doesn't work for you, then take the time to develop your own. My bowhunting revolves around deer and turkey hunting, so I've designed my worksheets with that in mind. No matter what species of game you hunt, you can easily see that the critique worksheet can be adapted to any game animal. In the past, I kept all my critique worksheets in clear document protectors, and stored in a notebook binder. Then changed over to using a computer to scan and store them. Recently, I've been bitten by the tablet bug, and will be storing all future critiques on my iPad. If you've been thinking about getting a tablet, this might give you the justification you've needed to convince your wife that you really can't live without one. It's always helped me to have my hunting partner review my critique worksheets, especially if he or she participated in the hunt. Hunting partners usually are eager to offer constructive criticism when asked, and it always seems that two heads are better than one when trying to remember the location of landmarks, game sighted and other important details.

I've learned a lot over the years since that morning I tagged the six-pointer, mentioned at the beginning of this chapter. For a confidence builder, nothing can top taking your first deer with a bow. No one single factor has helped me improve as a bowhunter more than the critique worksheet, and I'm sure you'll find that if you try this method of analyzing your hunts, that your mistakes will be fewer and fewer.

You'll get a reputation for magically knowing where all the deer are, and you'll take more game without depending totally on luck and the suicidal deer.

Author's Notes

I recognize that there are a number of very good Apps available for the computer, smart phone, and tablet that will work extremely well for critiquing a hunt. Go with whatever system works for you. Hopefully, I've motivated you to start collecting and using data from your hunts. For me, when it comes to hunting, I tend to want to keep it simple.

I'm scouting for fruit on a persimmon tree. This one is close to a bedding area. Ideal! You can tell it's early in the bow season; check out the short sleeve shirt.

8

PERSIMMONS, THE SOUTHERN DEER CANDY

The evening was drawing to a close much quicker than I wanted it to. The stand I was in overlooked a cove on Georgia's beautiful Clarks Hill Lake. I watched two mature Canadian geese with their young, feeding in the back of the cove. My confidence was high. This was one of those stand situations that you just know in your gut will produce deer. The trail I was watching originated in a bedding area of young pines, then ran along a ridge and ended at the back of the cove under a grove of persimmon trees. The ground under the trees was dotted with ripe, orange persimmons, and it was obvious from how the ground was torn with tracks, that this was a real deer grocery-store hot spot.

My tree stand was placed within 15 yards of an early-season, scrape on the trail which led down to the persimmons. The feeling of serenity, wonderful smell of mature pines, and incredible scenery was interrupted by the sound of movement on the trail. As the doe came into view on the trail, I slowly positioned myself on the stand and readied my Heritage Archery recurve for the shot. She headed my way at a steady trot, which worried me, because I don't often attempt moving shots, even at very close range. I was debating on whistling at her to try to get her to stop under my stand, when a buck came over the rise, 40 yards behind the doe. The decision was an easy one. She went on down to the persimmon tree, and I concentrated on how to stop the buck for a chance at a shot. The doe urine I had sprinkled in the scrape did the job for me, and he went right to it. As he moved his foreleg forward to paw at the scrape, I sent the cedar, Grizzly-tipped arrow on its way. The feathers disappeared against the buck's side with a sound of arrow against hide. It was a good hit, and the small six-point traveled only 40 yards before collapsing, ending a very rewarding, early-season, southern bowhunt.

I'm convinced that the persimmon grove was the key ingredient that made this hunt successful. I went on this hunt with very little time to scout the area. Knowing that acorns were not yet dropping in quantity, I spent my time looking for persimmons. General knowledge of where to look for persimmon trees allowed me to find a real deer honey hole in a relatively short amount of time. Finding the new scrape on a major trail leading to the persimmons was an extra bonus that paid off. During the first few weeks of the deer season, before the acorns are falling in large numbers, persimmons attract deer like candy.

Like most bowhunters, I'd like to have more free time for scouting hunting areas. My pre-season scouting generally consists of three or four weekends before opening day, trying to cover as much ground as possible, looking for the best place to start the season. Work commitments always seem to prevent me from being able to roam the woods and fields year-round as I'd like. By searching for persimmons, my limited scouting time is quality time that will generally pay off.

Bowhunters rely heavily on lures and scents to help them obtain that up-close shot. Persimmons make the perfect, natural deer lure for that period before the rut, when hunting over food offers a good chance for success. Narrowing down the areas where you scout, and having a good idea of what deer sign will consistently produce deer becomes very important when your scouting time is cut short. The deer in my hunting areas love to eat ripe persimmons during the early bow season. Therefore, I spend most of my early season scouting, looking for ripe persimmon trees.

I enjoy shooting the recurve and longbow. My accuracy with stick-bows lies with shots less than 20 yards, consequently, I have to work hard to get the deer in close. Using knowledge of deer habits and general woods lore to try and figure out where the deer will be during a hunt can be extremely enjoyable. There is a great feeling of accomplishment and pride in your bowhunting skills when everything comes together, and the deer walks within a few feet of your stand or blind. The persimmon tree acts like a magnet to draw the deer within range. A successful hunting strategy, with or without an opportunity for a shot, can be a very rewarding experience.

The persimmon is a tree 50 to 100 feet in height, with ovate, oblong, taper-pointed, shining leaves, pale-yellow flowers, and an orange-colored, round or egg-shaped, succulent fruit, an inch or more in diameter. The fruit is very astringent when green, but is edible when mellowed. When the fruit is so ripe and soft that it looks wrinkled and almost spoiled, it tastes the best. Then, it tastes very sweet and has a rich, fruity flavor. It grows plentifully from Connecticut to Texas.

The persimmons may be served raw or used in preserves, and the pulp is used in pies, custards, ice-cream, and sauces. Indians made a kind of bread by mixing mashed persimmon pulp with crushed corn. My experience has been that you should look for persimmon trees along the edges of fields, feed plots, clear cuts, roads, and shorelines. They seem to need a lot of sunshine. You're not likely to find them growing where the sunlight is blocked by larger trees. It has been my observation that the persimmon trees in my area only produce fruit every other year. In order to make my scouting easier, I keep a good log of persimmon tree locations in my hunting areas and which trees produced fruit. Be careful to follow the game laws when hunting persimmons growing along roads or shorelines. Most states require the hunter to be a specified distance from roads and water.

I've also found that when hunting directly over the persimmon tree, the majority of your shots will be at does. The bucks tend to hang back, waiting for the cover of darkness, before approaching, while the does and their young can often be seen standing on their hind legs to reach the low-hanging persimmons. Once you have located a persimmon tree with fruit, look for a major trail leading to the tree. If you find a single, major trail, scout the trail to see if it leads to a bedding area, or to a point where other minor trails feed into it. Setting up close to a bedding area, or near the intersection of trails leading to persimmons, usually is the best tactic for success. Quite often, fresh scrapes and rubs can be found along these major trails, and can offer an excellent chance to tag a buck. I like to build a mock scrape on a major trail leading to a persimmon tree, and have found that both bucks and does will almost always stop to scent check a new scrape. A hunting partner of mine, who was at first skeptical of using mock scrapes for fear of contaminating the area with human scent, recently tagged a nice buck and a fat doe using this technique, and now always uses mock scrapes when hunting trails leading to persimmons.

Bowhunting over a persimmon tree that is dropping ripe fruit in a deer-populated area, certainly should increase your chances of seeing game, and offers an excellent chance to tag a doe. Most southern states encourage you to harvest does. Georgia gives you tags that can only be used during the archery season, and only for the harvesting of does. For the new bowhunter who has doubts about his ability to tag a deer with his bow, hunting over persimmons should offer a lot of shots at deer, with an increased chance to break-the-ice with their first bow kill.

The next time you scout your hunting area, keep a look out for hot-spot persimmon trees, so that you, too, can enjoy heavy, bowhunting action over "Southern Deer Candy."

This buck came to a persimmon tree at first light. I shot him a few miles back in the brush and it was quite a chore dragging him out and crossing a creek with him, by myself.

*"What was big was not the antlers, but the chance.
What was full was not the meatpole but the memory
of the hunt."*

~ Aldo Leopold - Paraphrased ~

Can you find my tree stand in the picture?

This is a great example of a buck staging area. I know it looks like a bedding area, but it's actually on the edge of a swamp about 100 yards from the core bed area. Bucks feel comfortable and safe here and will use the thicket as a staging area waiting for dark. They're traveling through late in the evening and coming back in the morning on their way back to the bed.

9

HUNTING IN THE THICK OF IT

I could hear the rustle of the leaves as the deer moved around the cove toward my stand. By the sounds, the deer were moving at a good clip across the open sections of the mature pines. It was late morning. Other hunters would be out of their stand and wandering the woods, pushing deer into the bedding area thicket. There would not be any hope for a shot if the deer did not slow down before they came by me. I readied my bow in case one came in range, and as I heard them approach, disciplined myself not to look in their direction. I have always maintained that you should not make eye-to-eye contact with deer. Like man, they seem to have the uncanny ability to sense when they are being stared at. I spotted its antlers first, and then the buck appeared in the opening in front of me, just inside the briar packed staging area that I selected as an ambush site. The thicket was full of buck rubs and deer tracks. It was so thick that there was just one possible shooting lane; it was actually more of a hole to shoot down into than a lane. The deer was now merely ten yards away, and my dreams of tagging a nice buck with my longbow was very close to becoming reality.

Fundamental logic and a dash of good old common sense tells us that if you want to successfully hunt the whitetail, you must understand the behaviors of the deer well enough to try to think like one. The first-rate deer hunter has perfected this to a point of being able to enter the whitetails' world, not as an outsider to be wary of, but as another everyday curiosity. You must realize that the forest is the whitetails' living-room. They are very accustomed to every tree, bush, and smell of all the other animals in their area. Anything alien to what their senses consider to be normal will put deer into alarm mode. Once alarmed, deer will use survival methods that they have developed through time. They will limit their daytime movements and become nocturnal, and they will seek security in the thickest vegetation. This behavior enables them to survive and inhabit the outskirts of major cities in close proximity to man.

My military training taught me that surviving an escape and evasion situation hinges on your success at blending into, and becoming part of, your surrounding terrain. The mature buck is adept at this and can become essentially invisible by getting into the thickest brush and not moving. It is perhaps accurate to say that many hunters have almost stepped on deer they did not see until it hopped up from its hiding place. While hunting from a treestand, I have observed deer that lay concealed in a bush while a hunter walked within five feet of the deer without realizing its presence. The doe did not dare move for a long time after the hunter had disappeared down the trail. Then she stood up and went deeper into the thicket.

Putting all the data about whitetails to work for you in order to improve your hunting is very often an intimidating task due to the tremendous amount of information that has been discovered lately. My goal has always been to appreciate and know all I can about the abilities of an alarmed deer, and try to use the knowledge to my advantage. Understanding the significance of using wind direction, proper camouflage, masking, sex scents and techniques such as rattling, grunting, and building mock scrapes should be considered the essentials in deer hunting education. Even the best hunters will often alarm deer by leaving human scent, making alien noise, or by disrupting the areas' natural look. I believe that understanding what the deer will do once startled can become the ingredient necessary to increase your success as a deer hunter.

Deer search for security all the time. They react to what is going on in their immediate surroundings in order to survive. Coyotes; and other predators; also keep deer nervously seeking security. Use a topographical map to study the hunting area, and look at the map from the deer's perspective. Deer always want to feel safe; where would you feel safest if you were a deer? Where might you be capable of eluding predators? A turkey will roost elevated on a tree limb at night. All day long, the turkey is on the ground and on high alert for predators. When evening comes, the flock can go to roost where they can rest and feel safe. Obviously, a deer can't roost in a tree, but they seek the same safety as the turkey---they can get into the thickest, most impenetrable part of the woods.

It is my experience that once you identify the thickets, swamp bottoms, and briar patches in your hunting area, you will have found where deer spends most of their time---their bedroom. A buck does not just disappear off the face of the earth during the day, and then magically reappear in the early morning or late evenings. They are bedded down in the thickest part of woods they can find. A great way to harvest a trophy buck is to hunt just inside the edge of their bedroom. Even during the day, a buck will move very short distances within a thicket to change beds, follow a doe, chew on briar, and find water. A deer will feel safest in the thickest part of a swamp bottom where possibly no hunter has ever stepped foot.

For many years, I have enjoyed tremendous success hunting in the thickets. A valuable skill for bowhunting the buck's bedroom is an understanding of deer and wildlife behavior, basically to think like a deer. Knowing where other hunters may be in the area is another valuable bowhunting skill.

If you are bothered by getting covered up with mosquitos, ticks, poison ivy, no-see-ums, spiders, and snakes, then thicket hunting is not for you. Hunting the swamps, briar patches, and thickets can be difficult and get very uncomfortable. For this reason, most hunters will shy away from these areas. If you are a bowhunter, then you have already made the decision to take on the challenge, and hunt the hard way. Consistently harvesting a trophy buck with a bow requires "kicking things up a notch," going above and beyond what other hunters are willing to do.

A lot of my bowhunting has been on Fort Gordon, Georgia. The army base has large training areas for active and retired military personnel to hunt in. Many of the hunting areas are set aside for bowhunting only. There is a central location where all hunters must sign in and out of the area they are hunting. I spend a lot of time studying the sign-out sheets and maps to see where other hunters are headed. You cannot control where others will hunt in your area, so it is best to use them to your advantage. Generally, hunters will not venture into the thickest part of the woods. They will want to place their stand in a location that is easy to get to, and where they can see anything that moves for miles. Most hunters will hunt a few hours in the morning, and then get down from their stand. Before going back to their truck they will walk around the area looking for deer tracks, scrapes, or rubs. You need to use this information to your advantage. Hunters moving through the woods from 9 a.m. to noon will push deer that have been out feeding all night, back into the thickets as well as cause deer that are bedded to get on their feet and move. Look for swampy, creek bottom thickets that other hunters would be reluctant to venture into. Late in the winter is a great time to search for these buck sanctuaries. After the hunting season has ended the vegetation is not as thick, and it is easier to get into the thickets to look for deer sign and locate a stand site for next year.

I look for thick areas on the outer perimeter of thickets, called a buck staging area. Staging areas are where bucks will move late in the evening prior to dark, just before venturing out in the open to feed. What you hope to find is a staging hot-spot that is loaded with buck rubs. Rubs are a signpost---a visual sign that a buck creates so other deer will know he is using the area. They also scent mark the tree by rubbing a scent gland in their forehead into the rub. The thick young trees and saplings that grow close together in a thicket are a favorite for a buck to rub, because they are easy to rub and push against.

Scout the edges of thickets to look for staging areas and trails leading in and out of thick bedding areas. If possible, stay out of the center of the bedding area to minimize the amount of human scent and disturbance. Make sure you wear knee-high rubber boots and masking scent even when scouting. Do not scout or move into a thicket on days when the wind is moving in the direction of the thicket. A cross wind is the best for scouting or hunting trophy bucks. My experience has been that a mature whitetail buck will often travel with the wind from behind. It can see and hear everything in front and use its incredible nose to check anything from the rear.

Once I find a promising staging area, I will identify a tree for a stand site. Using a trail camera to scout the thicket is an excellent way to determine buck movement and best stand placement. Most of the time, vegetation and young trees will be so thick that you will not have a shooting lane at all. Keep in mind that things will look different from 18--20 feet up, and there might be holes in the brambles that you can shoot through. Take a portable pruning saw with you and create a small shooting lane. Be careful not to remove too much and destroy any chance of the buck continuing to use the area. All vegetation you cut down should be moved clear of the area to make sure all changes look as natural as possible. Hang your stand and use glow-in-the-dark tacks to mark the entry path to your stand.

Now, back to the approaching deer at the beginning of the chapter. The buck's body was so well camouflaged in the thicket that I could not make out which direction it was facing. It stood there for what seemed like quite a while, only moving its head, and its rack blended into the extremely thick patch of briar and young trees. When its head moved, it looked like the limbs in the thicket were moving. I was twenty feet up, standing with my longbow ready. I had a home-made cedar arrow nocked. The buck had to move in my direction and step into the one hole in the thicket that I could shoot into. On the way into the stand, I used a drag rag loaded with doe-n-heat scent and hung it in the small shooting hole. There was a very slight breeze blowing towards the buck. If it picked up my scent, I would be busted and probably never see it again.

The buck stood still for a long time; it was looking like it might bed down right where it was. I needed to get its attention and try to make something happen. My rattling antlers were dangling on a limb next to me, so

Chapter 9 – Hunting in the thick of it

I slowly hung my longbow on the bow hanger and reached for them. I was hoping that since I could not see the buck very well, that it would not be able to see any slight movement I made using the antlers. If I took my eyes off of the buck, it would be difficult to relocate its position. The buck was in a very dense part of the thicket, roughly twenty-five yards away. Its rack and body were not in full view yet, so I did not know if it was a shooter.

It was now or never! I lightly clicked the rattling antlers together just loud enough to get its attention, then used my mouth to grunt a couple of times. The buck spun his head around to look in my direction, and I froze. It completely turned around, and I could now see that he had been facing away from me the entire time. As it turned, I got my bow back in my hand, and situated myself to shoot. I had no idea how the buck was able to move through the amazingly thick vegetation, but it moved its head from side to side and jumped over dead falls as it came my way. The buck was definitely a shooter! I got a quick glimpse of high rack that looked to be at least four good points on one side. I don't like trying to count antler points when a deer is approaching. Take a quick glance at the rack to help you make a decision about harvesting the deer, then focus on picking a spot for the shot without making any mistakes.

Things started to happen quickly. The buck was under my stand; it was so close that I would have to look straight down to see it. It was obviously wondering what happened to the buck it had heard. If you've ever had a nice buck directly under your stand, then you would know how nerve racking it is. I felt like I did not dare breathe. Any noise from me or my stand, and it would be gone. I thought it would never move! My knees were beginning to tremble, and I had to concentrate to calm down. The last thing I needed at this point was a case of buck fever.

Then the buck finally moved towards the shooting hole. If it came through the brush in front of me and stepped towards the drag rag, it would be quartering away from me at about twelve yards. As the buck took the last few steps towards the drag rag, my bow came up. I picked a hair behind its shoulder, drew, anchored and let the arrow fly. The 160 grain snuffer tipped cedar arrow hit the spot where I aimed and knocked it down. The buck got up and took off, but it did not get far before getting tangled up in the briars. I sat down on the stand and tried to calm myself.

About ten minutes passed as I watched the buck for any sign of movement. It looked like he had taken his last breath. I was reflecting on the picture-perfect morning and how much I enjoy hunting the edge of the swamp, when I heard the distinct sound of antler rattling. My hearing was damaged in the military, and I frequently don't hear things until they are very near. The rattling was loud and close. Unbelievably, I did not even hear the two huge bucks approach the thicket behind me. They were apparently bedded close by. Perhaps they heard my rattling and came to investigate. I did not have another buck tag so shooting one of these brutes was not an option. Isn't that the way it always goes?

I quietly shifted around in the stand so that I could watch the action. Two bucks and a doe were roughly twenty-five yards from me in a very small opening in the thicket. From what I could see through the brambles and briars, a large bodied, long tined, eight-point buck was trying to shove a huge dark racked ten-pointer into the next county. Both wanted the doe for a girlfriend. The area was torn up with rubs, and now I know why. Obviously, a number of bucks were using this staging area on the edge of the swamp bedding area. The doe moved off deeper into the swamp and eventually both bucks chased after it. What a show! This encounter with nature is why I am out here, and why I will always be willing to take on the challenges and hard work involved with hunting the swampy bottoms and thickets.

This hunt got even more incredible. My buck still had not moved in over forty-five minutes, so I got out of the stand and went over to admire my trophy. Imagine my surprise when I saw that its rack was deformed on one side. My buck had a nice high four points on one side. On the other side, it had a deformed curved cow-horn spike with loads of sticker points at the base. I did not see any of this as it was moving through the thicket coming towards me. The deformed antlers did not bother me in the slightest. In fact, because my buck was so unique, it was even more of a trophy.

As I sat on the ground next to the buck, I kept thinking that I had seen it before. I could not shake the fact that something about this buck was very familiar. Its deformed rack was so distinctive that I knew there was no way I would forget this animal if I had seen it previously. Eventually, I stopped trying to figure out why my buck seemed so familiar, and started the work of dragging it to my truck. I took pictures and showed the buck off to my hunting buddies, who all thought he was a really cool and different trophy. The rack was so unique that I decided to mount it on an arrow-head shaped plaque. After processing the buck for the freezer, I placed the rack on a shelf in my shop to dry out.

Along with bowhunting, another passion of mine is shed antler hunting. Finding shed antlers will tell you that the buck has survived the previous season and also where he might still be spending a lot of time. I have found that the best places to look for sheds are the swamp bottoms and edges of thickets. For me, shed hunting and identifying staging area hotspots go together. Furthermore, roaming the woods in the dead of winter looking for sheds is the perfect time to pinpoint staging areas to hunt next Fall.

I have collected a lot of sheds over the years. I mark the really nice ones with the date and place where I found them. I keep most of my sheds on the shelves in my workshop, the same area where I went to place my new deformed buck rack to dry. As I went to lay this buck's rack on the shelf, I had to make some space for it. I moved some of the other sheds out of the way. Lo and behold! Propped up on a shelf was a cow-horned shed antler with lots of sticker points at the base. I found the shed on a swampy creek bank during the previous year's shed hunt in the staging area where I just tagged the weird antlered buck. The shed antler was so unique that there was no doubt that it belonged to this buck. No wonder the buck seemed familiar to me. What are the odds that I'd have the shed antler of this weird and unique trophy?

The weird rack is now mounted on a good-looking walnut arrowhead shaped plaque and hangs in a place of honor. On a shelf right next to it lay the shed. Each and every time I have an occasion to show off the trophies on my wall, the weird horned buck and its shed always invites the best storytelling, and gets the most attention. They are a testament to what you can find while hunting staging areas and swampy briar patches where no one else will go. So, get some decent bug spray and start kicking your bowhunting up a notch by "hunting in the thick of it."

I rattled and grunted this weird horned buck into range of my longbow while hunting in the thicket. What are the odds that I'd find his weird shed the previous year?

"A peculiar virtue in wildlife ethics is that the hunter ordinarily has no gallery to applaud or disapprove of his conduct. Whatever his acts, they are dictated by his own conscience, rather than by a mob of onlookers. It is difficult to exaggerate the importance of this fact."

~ Aldo Leopold - A Sand County Almanac ~

Nothing's as pretty as cedar arrows with a recurve bow. Unless its cedar arrows with a recurve bow leaning against a large buck rub!

10

CEDAR
~Do-It-Yourself Arrows~

Looking for a hobby to carry you over between your state's big game seasons? Of course there's small game hunting, target archery and bowfishing. For the do-it-yourselfer, I say there's nothing quite so pleasing and fulfilling as building your own arrows. Here's how to build cedar arrows, plus a look at the range of tools and supplies available to arrow building enthusiasts.

I'm the type of guy who enjoys fishing from the bank with crickets, worms and possibly, a cane pole The art of relaxing while fishing means more to me than catching a fish…although it's nice to catch one once in a while. For me, keeping it simple keeps it relaxing.

I'm also the type of guy who enjoys shooting cedar shafts from a longbow. Again, keeping it simple is important to me, and putting together my own arrows not only keeps it simple, but is a large part of the joy of archery.

Where I live, the central Savannah River area of Georgia, more bowhunters are choosing the recurve or longbow every year. In most cases, these same bowhunters are opting to shoot cedar. For years I used Easton's aluminum arrows for both target shooting and bowhunting, with excellent results, but now I shoot only cedar when using traditional gear.

It's possible you have thought about going to the recurve or longbow, and that you might also like to shoot cedar, but can't bring yourself to make the change. If you feel a need for something more from archery than you're getting, then perhaps the rewarding experience of putting together a dozen matching cedar arrows is what you're looking for. If you already shoot wooden shafts and aren't putting them together yourself, then I think you're missing out on a part of archery that will make you even prouder of your successes as a bowhunter. It's a special feeling knowing that the arrow that just got your deer was made by you just for that purpose. Also, if there's a young archer in the family, arrow-smithing can become a great way to spend quality time with your youngsters.

Through much trial and error I have developed a simple, inexpensive method of putting together handsome and functional cedar arrows in which I take great pride. You only need a few tools, some of which can be found around the home or purchased from local retailers.

Arrowsmithing

My arrowsmithing method is divided into three easy steps. First, correctly spined (arrow stiffness) shafts are cut to the proper length. Second, the shaft is prepared; this includes staining, painting, and cresting. Then the fletching and point are applied.

Blank Port Orford White Cedar shafts can probably be purchased through your local archery retailer, or from any number of dealers that you can find advertising in "Traditional Bowhunter" magazine. I have used ACME premium shafts for years, and find that their shafts make a top-notch arrow. It's important that you purchase shafts that are spined correctly for the bow that you intend to shoot. I prefer to use shafts spined at least 10 pounds heavier than the bow I'm shooting. This insures a good flying arrow that needs little if any tuning to the bow. It will also help compensate for the bad release that always seems to happen at the worst possible time. I do not recommend shooting cedar arrows from any compound bow, no matter how stiff the arrows are spined. They might fly just fine, but the modern compound bow releases enough energy to possibly shatter a cedar arrow, causing serious injury.

When the longbow or recurve is canted, a wide variety of shaft sizes can be shot from a properly tuned bow. Once you have purchased blank shafts in the proper spine, you're ready to cut them to your draw length. Blank cedar shafts generally are sold 32 inches long. To determine your proper draw length (arrow length), take an uncut blank shaft and using a taper tool, taper one end to receive a nock. An inexpensive taper tool works like a pencil sharpener, and can be purchased at your local archery shop. Draw your bow a number of times or shoot a few arrows so that you are consistently pulling to the same anchor point. Nock the bare shaft to the string, and after you have drawn and anchored have someone mark the shaft approximately ½ to 1 inch in front of the bow. This will allow clearance for your fingers if you grip the bow with a closed hand. Now you can use this shaft as a guide to measure and cut others. I like to use heavy duty rubber bands to tie a dozen shafts together; then using a miter box I cut them all at once – that way they are all exactly the same length. After you cut them to the proper length, use a tapering tool to taper the point and nock end of all the shafts. Working the complete dozen a step at a time will give you a more evenly matched set of arrows than if you worked each arrow individually.

A quiver full of custom cedar arrows. These were made for me by a bowhunting friend after receiving a few arrowsmithing lessons. You will be surprised how tuff and long-lasting a cedar arrow is. I have arrows that I made over twenty years ago that are still straight and ready to hunt.

If you plan to paint the entire shaft, it's important at this time to identify the section of shaft where the grain is closest together. This is the stiffest section of the shaft and, to get the most out of the spine of the shaft, this section should be placed against the sight window of the bow. You need to do this now because later you'll need this for correct placement of the nock on the shaft. Once the arrow is completely painted you can't see the grain. Put a mark on the point end of the shaft so that it identifies the section of the shaft where the grain is the tightest. Make the mark on the end of the shaft and not on the taper. The taper might be painted, which would cover up the mark. If you don't plan to paint the entire shaft, then marking the shaft is not necessary because you can check the grain tightness later. You can also check the grain later if you decide to use a stain on the shafts. Before you go crazy trying to make up your mind what color paint or shade of stain to use, you first must prepare the shafts to be stained or painted. Wet the shafts lightly with a damp rag, just enough to dampen the outer fibers. Then set them aside to dry. This will cause all the loose surface fibers to stand up. Now, using fine steel wool or very light fine sandpaper, lightly rub the shafts until they're silky smooth. This should take only light rubbing. You don't want to decrease the diameter of the shaft to the point of affecting the spine.

Now you must decide how you want to finish your arrow shafts. This depends on how you plan to use the arrows. A camo or stain finish might be what you want for hunting arrows – a much brighter finish for target arrows. It's a matter of personal preference. When tree stand hunting I use arrows painted with a bright color, because it helps identify the location of a hit on a deer, plus the deer isn't as likely to pick out any bright colored movement up in a tree. I feel camo shafts are a must for turkey hunting and

I also feel more confident using camo painted shafts when hunting deer from the ground. Whether or not deer see bright colors is still debatable, so when hunting at their eye level, why take any chances?

Shades of stains and colors of paint are limited only to your imagination. I like wood stain that is normally used for gunstock finishing, but any inexpensive furniture stain will work just fine.

There are two ways you can go when painting your shafts: Dipping the shafts using a dip tube, or spray painting them using an aerosol spray paint. If you plan to dip the shafts, Fletch-lac is your best bet. It comes in a wide variety of colors, including fluorescents, and along with a dip tube can normally be purchased at your local archery shop or traditional archery supplier. I personally like to spray paint my shafts using inexpensive automotive lacquer. Most auto parts stores carry auto touch-up lacquer in a wide assortment of colors. You waste a little more paint spraying rather than dipping the shafts, but I feel I get a more even coat, and in most cases one or two coats is enough. I've also used inexpensive spray enamels with good results as long as they're over coated with a clear polyurethane.

You can enhance the eye appeal of your arrows by using a cresting tool, which spins the shafts at a set speed so that a precise line of brightly colored paint can be applied. It's fun to develop your own cresting color code which will add a personal touch to your arrows. Commercial cresting lacquers are available in many colors. However, I have found that model airplane enamel, which can be purchased at any toy store, works well as long as you protect the shaft with a polyurethane finish.

One of the nice things about using cedar is that it's so inexpensive you can afford to experiment until you find what's right for you.

My favorite all-around arrow is stained a pine straw color, then spray painted with fluorescent orange lacquer nine to ten inches at the nock end. After applying a cresting of two ¼ inch wide yellow bands bordered with thin black bands, the entire shaft is finished with either a clear lacquer or clear polyurethane. Add five inch yellow feathers and you have an arrow that is easy to spot on the side of a deer, but hard to lose in the grass.

The last thing you need to do before fletching your shafts is to apply the nock. Remember to put the nock on the shaft so the section of shaft with the tightest grain will be against the sight window of the bow. If you can't see the grain through the paint, then use the mark you made earlier to align the nock in the right place. Otherwise, look at the grain and align the nock correctly. Again, it is important to keep the stiffest section of the shaft against the bow in order to get the full benefit from the spine of the arrow. Use nocks sized for the diameter of the shafts, 23/64 inch or 11/32 inch.

There are many types of adhesives that will work well when applying nocks to cedar. Fletch-Tite, Duco cement or any of the new fletching and super glues designed to adhere to wood are a good choice. If you have a cresting tool, use it to spin your arrow and insure that your nock is aligned properly before the glue sets. If the nock spins true without any wobble, then it's on correctly.

The fletching or guidance system for the arrows comes in two types, feathers or vanes. I highly recommend that when shooting off the shelf of a bow you use feathers. They flatten out and give more than vanes will and won't cause the arrow to kick away from the bow when the fletching encounters the sight window. Vanes have the advantage of being water-proof. They fly great when shot off an adjustable arrow rest such as those that are standard equipment on most compound bows, but just don't perform well for me when I use a recurve or longbow. For broadhead flight, a five inch, three fletch guidance system is hard to beat. I have found that cedar arrows fletched with Maxi-Fletch feathers by Trueflight fly extremely well. Feathers are either right-wing or left-wing. It makes no difference which you use as long as your fletching jig uses the same clamp and you use the same type on each arrow. You can purchase fletching jigs from your local archery shop in two types, mono-fletchers (which put one feather or vane on at a time) or multi-fletchers (which put all three feathers or vanes on at a time). Feathers come in many colors. They are normally purchased by the dozen or by the hundred and, except for barred feathers, are fairly inexpensive. Using a fletching jig, apply your feathers to the shafts using a good adhesive such as Fletch-Tite or Everfast cement; both come in a tube and are easy to use. I've found you get more stability from your arrows if you fletch them ¼ inch from the nock.

Once you have the fletching in place you're ready to finish your arrows by applying the point. Use either broadheads or field points that are tapered for the shaft diameter. I like to use 160 grain field points for target practice, which can easily be replaced with 160 grain Snuffer broadheads for hunting. The Hot Melt adhesive that comes in the stick form works best for me when putting any type of point on a cedar shaft. Use your cresting tool to spin the arrow and check for proper point alignment the same way you did for the nock.

You now have a dozen handsome and durable cedar arrows that anyone would be proud to shoot. Arrowsmithing can be much more detailed, but this will give you a place to start. It's an inexpensive and productive hobby. If you're like me, making cedar arrows will be a very enjoyable way to spend rainy weekends and hot summer days when you are normally just daydreaming about hunting.

Go ahead. Make the change to keeping it simple, while adding to the challenge. This could be the season that you experience the self-satisfaction of taking your buck with an arrow made from naturally beautiful cedar, which for a lot of us brings back memories of a simpler time. *The more your equipment reflects how you feel about the sport of bowhunting, the better bowhunter you'll be.*

Making cedar arrows at the kitchen table

"I don't believe in the separation of archers by the type of equipment we use. Only that we all share in the enjoyment of a great sport, and should continue to stick together for the preservation of archery."

~ Ralph Blackwelder ~

Making Woodies Poem

~ unknown author ~

Another summer has passed away; another field has gone to hay.

It's close to season, another reason, for making Woodies.

The broadheads filed, the shavings piled, the nuts are falling....the squirrels are wild;

No need to reason....tis' just the season, for making Woodies.

When you have got the fever, there's nothing that works as good;

As gathering nocks and fletching, and working with shafts of wood....

So go ahead, and set the clamp; you need some Scotchgard...in case it's damp.

No need to reason, we need no season, for making Woodies.

Columbia County, Georgia - #1 Pope & Young Record – harvested by
the author on November 1, 2009

11

THE COLUMBIA COUNTY MONSTER

~New P & Y record bow harvest for Columbia County, GA~

I n 2009, I lived in rural Georgia and good hunting land was a short walk from my front door. Surrounded by hundreds of acres of woods and farm land, I lived a stone's throw from woodlots full of white oak and hardwood groves, swampy bottoms, and plenty of head-high thickets.

Sometimes, even when a hunter does all the things the experts swear will work, he finds bowhunting success comes more from luck than anything else.

As the years have gone by, each one quicker than the last, my hours and days spent in the woods, and tree stand have become fewer. Life seems to have a way of interfering, and finding time for things we love and the things that really should be a priority in life can become difficult as we get older.

Medical problems kept me from bowhunting during September 2009. The weather was unusually hot and dry, even for Georgia. I have always found it difficult to stay on stand for extended periods when the sweat is running down my face and the "no-see-ums" are eating me alive. As the rut approached, I spent most of my time checking the known honey holes in my hunting area for fresh scrapes, rubs, and doe activity. I'm a huge believer in the saying: "Find the does, and the bucks won't be far behind." I like to concentrate on finding the favorite food sources for the deer in the area, especially those sources that are close to bedding areas. White oak acorns that are dropping, dogwood berries, or persimmons are key food items that always get a lot of doe activity here in Georgia.

As October ended, I still did not see many deer in the usual high-traffic doe dining rooms. I was battling medical problems and could not hunt or scout often. When I did get in a stand, I could not sit very long and rarely saw much in the way of deer activity. I was frustrated because I knew that there was a good population of deer in the areas I was hunting. My trail cameras were filled with late-night pictures of mature does feeding on white oak acorns.

During the last week of October, I spent my time looking for signs of bucks looking for does. I had harvested a nice nine-point buck a few years prior and never expected to see a buck much larger than that. Most of the available hunting land is either wildlife management land or hunt club controlled land. Columbia County, Georgia is not known for record book whitetails, because too many bucks are harvested before they ever reach record-book trophy size.

I have always felt that any deer harvested with legal bow hunting equipment is a trophy. I have lost count of how many deer I have harvested with a bow and arrow, and prior to 2009, never gave any thought to having any of them measured for a record book. My love for the hunt and simply being in the outdoors has always been the true reward for me. The memories of the hunt, of the ones that got away, of the arrow sailing just over the back of a huge buck after glancing off a small unseen branch, of a lifetime of

Chapter 11 – The Columbia County Monster

becoming one with wildlife and nature have all been forever annotated in the personal "record book" of my soul.

I was scheduled to go with my wife, Lisa, to Atlanta the weekend of 1 November. With only a day or two to scout and hunt before the trip, I planned to concentrate on an area in the white oaks with signs of recent buck activity. The area had all the elements I continually look for; an open pasture area bordered by a thicket being used as a travel funnel between a bedding area and a white oak ridge with lots of does visited the oaks. The week before, I found several very large fresh rubs and a fresh scrape that was full of big tracks. I placed my trail camera pointing down the trail leading from the scrape to the white oak grove and left the area alone for a few days so that I would not pressure any bucks looking for does.

I sat on stand from before first light until around 11AM that last Friday of October. Just as on previous hunts that fall, deer movement during legal hunting hours was almost non-existent. A couple of does came by to feed on the acorns littering the area, but there was no sign of the buck that made the rubs and scrape. Before going back to the house, I took the memory card from a trail cam. To this point, this camera had only captured does, fawns, and raccoons. The camera also had occasional pictures of my neighbor who visited my stand placements in his John Deere Gator to enjoy the woods. Of course, his visits more-than-likely left unwanted scent on the trails, adding an extra level of difficulty to my hunting.

Once I got back to the house, I immediately checked the memory card. The card had about ninety pictures because I had set the camera to take a picture every minute. I scrolled through the pictures slowly, enjoying some close ups of does and spike bucks munching on acorns and a family of raccoons walking the trail single file.

My scrolling through the pictures stopped at picture number sixty four. I froze in my chair. Monster bucks like the one I was seeing did not roam the woods in Columbia County. I was looking at close ups of a sure thing record book buck.

It didn't make sense that a deer this size had never been spotted by anyone. There are a lot of hunt clubs throughout the county and a buck this size would not stand a chance surviving on hunt club property. He obviously has stayed close by, moved at dark, and spent most of his life in the thickets. I am also a shed hunter and have never found sheds in this area that come anywhere close to the size this buck was wearing.

I went into full buck hunting battle mode. I was determined to use all my years of experience and hunting skills to harvest this brute. My plan was to stay on stand as much as possible through the weekend. I was worried about how to tell my wife she would be going to Atlanta alone. But, after she saw the trail cam photo and how excited I was, she knew I had to stay home and hunt.

Friday night I washed all my hunting clothes in baking soda for scent control and also scrubbed my knee-high rubber boots with baking soda. I was up long before first light and after showering with baking soda, and getting my gear together, I headed for the stand in the white oak grove. The wind direction was crosswind from the direction I thought the buck would come from, which was exactly like I wanted it. It was overcast with light but steady rain. Even though I had been hunting long enough to know that the odds of my seeing the big buck were slim, I was pumped. I knew he lived somewhere not far off, it was the peak of the rut, and mature does were feeding in the oak grove. I was ready to hunt him as hard as I knew how.

It rained all day. I stayed on stand until legal hunting time ended. Not a single deer came down the trail. No animals of any kind came by. Could I have left my scent in the area by over-hunting? Had my neighbor or someone else been roaming the woods and spooked the monster? By the time I got home, I wondered if I would ever see the huge buck.

I spent that evening beating myself up over not going to Atlanta with Lisa. She is my "Other Half" and we do everything together. As her husband, maybe I should have gone with her instead of wasting time hunting in the miserable rain for a buck that I'd probably never see again – even on the trail cam. Maybe I should just get in the truck and head to Atlanta now? I could be there in two hours. These are the questions I was asking myself on Saturday, the last day of October.

I didn't go to Atlanta, but I didn't sleep very much either. The trail camera picture kept invading my thoughts as I tried to drift off. After a long night, I got up very early. I'm not much good without that first cup of coffee. My lower back, butt, and feet were sore from the long sit and climbing into the stand the day before. I was not looking forward to another long day with no deer movement. Fortunately, I fought the urges and got my gear together and headed out for the stand well before first light. My wind direction powder indicated a slight swirl that had me worried from the minute it got light enough to see out past twenty yards. The rain had stopped and the woods were quiet, except for the sounds of the last of the rain dripping from the leaves of the trees.

Due to arthritis I developed from years of longbow and recurve shooting, I switched from my longbow to a modern compound bow the previous year. The compound allows me to hunt using a light-weight bow and I don't need to practice as much to have the high level of confidence that I demand from myself. My 55# Mathews Drenalin bow was hanging on the bow hanger with an arrow nocked and ready. Because of the medical problems I have had, I could not stand for long. I was sitting facing the trail that led back toward the bedding area and scrapes. I had practiced shots from a sitting position and was confident that I could make the shot if the buck came within 20 yards.

Before climbing up in the stand, I placed canisters of doe-n-heat scent in a couple of shooting lanes. It was light enough for me to see the canisters hanging on the branches. After the first few hours of daylight passed without any deer activity, I started thinking about going back home. As I talked myself into staying, I felt encouraged by the sounds of a turkey hen yelping on a distant ridge. I knew I would never bag a prize buck from the sofa. I had faith that if I could last long enough, something good would happen.

My eye caught movement through the trees in front of me. I saw the line of an animal's back, but I thought it might be a horse from one of the pastures. It was too far to tell. Even though I couldn't tell what the animal was, I knew I had to get ready. Slowly, I reached for my bow and moved into position. Hunters who wait to get into position until a deer is in range go home empty handed. After what seemed like a quarter of an hour, but was probably more like a minute or two, the deer moved. It was the monster!

Chapter 11 – The Columbia County Monster

What are the odds of this happening? Will anyone believe that I saw this deer? Am I dreaming? This can't be happening! Where's my camera when I need it? The buck moved to within thirty yards, and was out in front of me, looking in the direction of a large scrape. I was hoping that the scent canisters would hide any of my scent that might be swirling his way and that the doe-n-heat scent would bring him closer. I had the bottom of my bow resting in the top of my rubber boot and was actually using the bow limb to hide my face. I was in position and ready to draw and shoot. This is the moment when experience and luck come together. Predicting what a deer will do is almost impossible, but experience will give you tools to use when in this situation, and can also help you stay calm and focus when "Buck-Fever" gets a hold on you. Experience lessens the chances of making mistakes.

I knew that for any chance at a shot, he must come closer. He started moving through the woods away from me and towards the scrape. I am pretty good at grunting with my mouth and didn't feel that I'd spook him with a grunt. It was time to make something happen I took a couple of deep breaths and quickly ran through my mental checklist; arrow is on the rest, wind is good, no other deer around, bow limb is clear of any obstructions, concentrate on picking-a-spot, don't lock eyes with him, and absolutely no looking at the rack. You need to answer only one question: Is the deer a shooter or not? A quick glance at the body and rack and you'll know. Focus on where you are going to place your shot, not on how many points he has.

My mouth opened and I grunted and snort wheezed at him. It worked! Here he comes! OMG I'm going to get a shot! He's moving down the trail right at me. As his head goes behind a large pine, I come to full draw and settle the string against the tip of my nose. I need him to turn and he does. Putting his nose against a scent canister, he is broadside at 15 yards. Concentrate! Now! Pick the spot - behind the shoulder - a little low. As soon as the arrow left the bow, I knew the shot was good. He fell to the ground, jumped up, stood still for a second, and then took off through the woods staggering. I heard him crash and after picking out a landmark in that direction, I made sure that my safety strap was still tight to the tree. I was shaking and didn't want to end up falling from the stand.

This is why I've been a hunter all my life and what *The Bowhunting Life* and experience is all about. Weeks, days, and hours of sitting and hunting hard can become the adrenaline-pumping thrill of a lifetime. I love it! Don't start bowhunting if you have a weak heart. A bowhunting encounter with a huge whitetail will get your heart racing faster than any equipment they have at the Y.

After a lifetime of hunting, I knew what a miracle this buck was. There were so many things against this happening; I was supposed to go to Atlanta with Lisa, I almost gave up yesterday after sitting in the rain all day, I almost went back to bed, I almost got out of the stand early because I wasn't seeing deer movement. What an incredible hunt! I was in the right place at the right time. When the monster showed up, I was lucky that he turned the right way and experienced enough to stay calm and make the shot that I had made so many times in practice.

Once I was able to get myself calmed down and after about thirty minutes of nothing but quiet from the direction he ran, I gathered up my gear and got out of the stand. I knew exactly where he was standing when I shot, because he was right next to one of my scent canisters (this is not the first time that placing scent canisters around my stand has paid off). There was a good deal of blood where he fell, and I immediately found a great blood trail. I felt very confident that the arrow went where it needed to, and that he couldn't have gone very far. I decided to follow the blood trail.

I found the feather end of my arrow about thirty yards into the woods. I saw his rack sticking up out of some brush. The thrill of the moment was overwhelming. The one trail camera picture that I had was taken with him facing the camera and was a little out of focus, making it difficult to tell how many points he had. He was an absolutely gorgeous deer and, a real monster of a buck for this area of Georgia. My arrow hit him perfectly behind the shoulder (If you look closely, you can see a piece of my arrow still in the buck).

Lisa was still in Atlanta. I knew that she wouldn't believe it if I called her, so I turned on my cell phone and took a picture of the buck and sent it to her phone. Even with the picture, I don't think she believed it at first, but once it sunk in, we were both screaming and hi fiving over the phone. She wished that she were there to help me drag him out of the woods. We hung up and I called my hunting buddy and close friend Jim Timmerman (I call him Tim). I have known Tim ever since we served in the Army together and we are as close as brothers. I needed some help getting the monster back to the house and I knew Tim would help. Like Lisa, Tim thought I was kidding, until he saw the picture.

With Tim's help, we got the buck back to the house and on my skinning rack. Lisa and I process our own venison so I took my time and prepared the deer for the freezer and a trip to the taxidermist. After the required drying period, the rack was scored for Pope and Young records by two certified Georgia DNR employees and is now listed as the #1 bow harvest for Columbia County.

This truly was the hunt of a lifetime for this ole Georgia bowhunter and storyteller. The Columbia County Monster graces a special place in my home and in my heart, and it will provide me with special memories forever.

Truly... an unbelievable moment!

"Luck is what happens when preparation meets opportunity."

~ Seneca; Roman dramatist, philosophe (5 BC - 65 AD) ~

This ten-point fell to a 160 grain snuffer broadhead from my
home-made custom osage longbow.

12

TIPS FOR BOWHUNTING TROPHY BUCKS

Preparation:

- Wear knee high rubber boots (barn boots) for scent control.

- Wear camouflage clothing washed in baking soda (no perfumed detergents).

- Stay away from after-shave, gasoline, oil, cigarette smoke, perfume, garlicky foods, and cooking smells prior to hunting.

- Use full camouflage – including face net and gloves. Nothing should be shiny or shining.

- Use human cover scent (fox pee) on rubber boots prior to walking into your stand site. Also use cover-up, scent shield for body odor elimination.

- Use odorless bug repellant, "Muskol" works best for me.

- Use spray paint to camouflage your tree stand. Leave it outside for a few days to get rid of all paint odors. Do the painting before the start of the season!

Failure to do these basics will drive mature bucks to become totally nocturnal and untaggable.

The Stand:

- Use a light-weight portable climbing or hanging stand system for quick and quite movement of stands. I like hang-on stands with climbing stick systems the best.

- There should be no metal on metal (human generated) noise while putting up or taking down your stand. If necessary pad any noisy parts with foam padding that you can tape on with camouflage duct tape. Foam water pipe insulation works great.

- Hunt as high as you can, safely – while being able to shoot accurately. I prefer 18 – 20 feet. Clear any brush or limbs that will be in the way of a shot, but don't clear so much that things look unnatural. When in your stand, you should blend into the surroundings and have good background foliage to keep you from being observed.

- *__Always__* wear a safety strap while treestand hunting (including going up and coming down the tree). Stay strapped in while stepping from a step/ladder system on to your stand. Once both feet leave the ground you must stay strapped safely to the tree until back on the ground.

- Stalk your way into the stand – don't touch the brush or walk down deer trails. Wait until after first light, when you can see your way through the woods, if it helps you move quitter than moving in the dark. When possible, I avoid using a flash light to get to my stand. Lighting up the woods in an unnatural way disturbs all forest animals and alerts them to your presence. Take your time going to your stand. Any noise you make should sound natural, such as the noise a possum or squirrel might make scampering through the woods.

- *__Always__* pull your bow and arrows up. Don't climb with bow and arrows. Don't attempt to replace broadheads while in your stand. Replacing, sharpening, and working with broadheads should be done in a safe environment with both feet on the ground.

Lures:

- Use small canisters – for years, I used the old 35mm film canisters before digital cameras. Now you can purchase scent canisters from any store that carries hunting lures and supplies. Fill the canister with cotton balls. You can attach clothespins to the canisters if needed to easily attach to a branch. Soak the cotton balls with doe-n-heat lure. I like to hang lure canisters out around my stand in all directions - about three feet above the ground and out 10 – 15 feet from your stand in good shooting lanes. Prime the canisters with fresh lure every time you place them out.

- *__Don't__* place lure on the tree you're in or on yourself. Deer will come too close and probably see you before you can get off a shot. Place lure canisters where you want to shoot the deer. I learned this lesson the hard way many years ago. My thinking, at the time, was that by putting lots of doe-n-heat lure on my boots that a deer would follow me to my stand, and I'd get an easy kill. I got half of it right – about fifteen minutes after I got settled in my stand, a huge buck followed me and came right to me. The problem was that he actually licked the screw in tree steps I was using to climb the tree and then stood there at the base of the tree and looked right up at me. He eventually figured out that I didn't look anything like a doe-n-heat and bounded off – leaving me shaking and frustrated. I've never forgotten that lesson learned.

- Use a clean rag on a long string to make a drag rag. Wet the rag with doe-in-heat lure and drag it behind you as you're moving to your stand. Stop about fifteen yards from your stand in a shooting lane and hang the drag rag on a nearby branch. You might get a buck to follow the drag scent and give you a shot. Don't be afraid to use a lot of lure on the rag, and keep the drag rag in a zip lock bag when not in use.

Equipment & Shooting:

- ***Practice, Practice, Practice*** with the same equipment you will hunt with, especially the same arrow and broadhead. 3D targets are excellent. My practice range includes both a ground target and ladder stand with numerous 3D deer targets set up in realistic hunting postures.

- Practice shooting from your actual hunting tree stand. Always wear a safety strap! If you anticipate having to shoot from a sitting position, then practice shooting while sitting. You will find that accurately shooting while sitting takes a lot of practice.

- Practice shooting at small objects. This will help when you need to pick a small spot on a deer.

- Keep your equipment as simple as possible – there will be less to go wrong at a critical moment. If items added to your bow don't make it shoot significantly better, than remove them. If you keep a bow quiver on your bow while hunting, then make sure you have it on your bow during practice sessions.

- If you don't know how to tune your bow for good arrow flight, ask a local expert to teach you. Usually your local archery retailer will be able to assist. I like to use the paper tuning method. You can find paper tuning instructions by searching the Internet or YouTube.

The Shot:

- ___*Pick-a-spot !*___   Pick a hair on the lower ½ portion of the deer immediately behind the front shoulder. Don't shoot at the whole deer.

  I don't look at the antlers, or make prolonged eye contact with deer. Concentrate on a spot and wait for a good penetration angle.

- Don't shoot beyond your capability. If you're like me, 20 yards or closer.

- Be determined and confident. Confidence will grow with experience. A great confidence booster is to harvest does with your bow. When that trophy buck is working his way towards your shooting lane, you must focus all your energy on being determined to take that deer home with you. You must know without a doubt that you have the skills needed to make it happen.

- Envision a grapefruit size ball between and behind the front shoulder and shoot to hit the ball dead center. Total concentration on a small target is the key. Literally – pick a hair to shoot at. I use a permanent ink marker to write "pick-a-hair" on the feather end of my arrow. This acts as a reminder every time I glance over at my bow with arrow nocked hanging on the bow hanger.

- Wait for the right moment to shoot, but don't hesitate once that moment arrives. You need a shot that will provide the best chance for a clean kill. We owe it to the animal not to shoot until we know that we can make a good, humane shot. At the same time, the longer a deer stays in front of your stand, the better chances are he'll pick up your scent and you'll be busted.

- Develop a mental checklist – a countdown of things to check prior to drawing your bow on a deer. Your checklist might include; is my arrow on the rest, are the bow limbs clear of any obstruction, are there other deer close by, etc.... Using a mental checklist will counter some of the effects of buck fever by helping to get your mind off the buck and his antlers. This has always been an invaluable tool for me. It works to calm me down and limits any mistakes.

There is probably no better way to practice than roaming through the woods stump shooting. I like to use judo points for shooting at stumps, eaves, sticks, pinecones......

Rub & Scrape hunting:

- Fresh tracks and rubs tell where a buck has been, but a fresh scrape tells where a buck will be.

- The earliest rubs are generally made by the local dominant buck.

- Pecking order scrapes (generally boundary scrapes) are early September scrapes the local bucks use to determine dominance.

- Breeding scrapes created later in the fall are used year after year by numerous bucks to locate local does in heat.

- For trophy bucks, it's best to focus your hunting on the breeding scrapes.

- A rub line can tell you the travel pattern of a buck, but scrapes are where you should concentrate your efforts.

- Don't touch a scrape without rubber gloves. Don't sit on the ground anywhere near your stand. Don't urinate near your stand.

- During the early season, hunt in areas where primary food sources are abundant. Acorns (white oaks – the best), persimmons, muscadines, honeysuckle, crabapple, etc…

- Locate food sources closest to a bedding area without disturbing bedded deer. Stay at least 75 yards from the bed.

- Always incorporate rattling and grunting into your bowhunting. Rattling is a long distance attractor. I normally don't grunt unless I see the deer. Grunting can maneuver deer in for a shot and is a great close range attractor. Practice grunting without a grunt call. Use your mouth, and try to make grunt sounds that come close to what the grunt call makes. You will be surprised at how good you'll get at grunting and it is one more tool in your bag of skills you might need to take a trophy buck. When you're at full draw, and the buck of a lifetime is at fifteen yards and walking away from you, grunt with your mouth. You have nothing to lose.

- In my experience, the very best rattling time is the last two weeks in October through mid-November.

- Be versatile – change tactics and try new and different techniques. Try hunting at mid-day.

- Yelp & Cluck! When a buck is in range but there is no shot offered or the buck is obviously nervous, use soft turkey calls to calm him down. Curiosity will often bring him in for that close shot. Deer will normally start feeding and relax when they hear turkey feeding clucks and purrs.

Wind & Thermals:

- I like to hunt with a crosswind from the direction I believe deer will be approaching. Bucks (4 ½ and older) often will move with the wind. Why? They use their eyes and ears for up front and their nose for detecting any threat from the rear. Again – cross wind hunting works!

- A mature buck will often let other deer act as sentry for them – only approaching once the others have moved by safely. If you want to tag a trophy, you must let the other deer pass by. The does and young bucks that you let pass by your stand will leave their scent for the monster to follow. Their scent will work to relax him when he comes down the trail past your stand.

- When hunting, constantly be aware of air thermals — air/scent will rise as the sun comes up and the day gets warmer. Bucks like to travel ridges in the morning. They use the rising air thermals to scent check everything below. The reverse is true in the evening. Air/scent will fall as the sun goes down and the day cools off in the evening. Bucks will often travel the base of ridges in the evening using the falling thermals.

- You can never totally hide your human scent, so you must also consider wind and thermals when scouting, still hunting, or stand hunting

Know your hunting area:

- Learn everything you can about the area you're hunting. Get a good overall picture of deer movement patterns in the area.

- Try and get an idea of the number of different family groups, including bucks associated with them.

- Know where the peak breeding areas are within this area. Know where to find the primary rut scrapes.

- Spend as much time as possible in the woods and in your stand. Hunt through lunch! Mature bucks will pattern a hunter's movement and move at noon.

- Use trail cameras to assist with identifying deer and wildlife in your hunting area.

Harvesting:

- Let the smaller and younger deer walk. Mature bucks are the last to come in to the stand site. They have learned to hang back in the comfort of the thick bedding area and generally only venture out if following a doe in heat or to check scrapes at dark.

- You will never harvest a monster buck if you are always shooting at the first deer that walks by.

- Always show respect for the animal by not shooting until you are 100% certain and confident of a clean and humane kill. I know that sometimes unfortunate things can go wrong even with the best intentions, but let's do everything possible to minimize the unfortunate incidents.

- Eat what you harvest and don't harvest outside of the legal limit or more than you plan to eat.

- If you don't know how to field dress and process your own deer, get someone to teach you. It's not difficult and the quality and quantity of the venison you put in your freezer will be far superior when you do it yourself.

I harvested this early season buck while hunting over
a favorite southern deer food - muscadines

CONCLUSION

It's now been over forty years since I took up archery and bowhunting. I guess you could say that roaming the outdoors with a bow & arrow is in my blood. The bowhunting life has always been something that I've never been able to get enough of. Bowhunting is a wonderful opportunity to get outdoors and enjoy wildlife and nature. You don't have to be a world-class archer, use a specific type of archery gear, or harvest a trophy animal, to live *the bowhunting life*. In this hectic digital world, we live in; it's more important than ever that we get away and enjoy outdoor activities.

Introduce someone to bowhunting, so we can keep bowhunting alive forever. Take a young person to the woods with you. Teach them to shoot a bow. Take them to a hunter safety class, and then take them hunting. Always be an ethical woodsman, respect the animal you hunt, and expect others to do the same.

A final comment - if you're a bowhunter and have never turkey hunted with a bow and arrow, you have no idea how much fun you're missing. Don't let another season go by without giving it a try. You can decide what the measurement of success is. Being on a ridge at first light and being able to enjoy the wildlife as the morning sun rises is as good as it gets. Hearing a turkey gobble, in the distance – is just icing on the cake

ALWAYS pick-a-spot!

Happy Bowhunting

"Go afield with a good attitude, with respect for the wildlife you hunt and for the forest and fields in which you walk. Immerse yourself in the outdoor experience. It will cleanse your soul and make you a better person."

~ Fred Bear (1902-1988) ~

ABOUT THE AUTHOR

Ralph Blackwelder has been an avid outdoorsman and bowhunter for over forty-five years. He started shooting recurve bows as a teenager, changed to compounds with the Jennings TStar, then started shooting and building his own longbows in the mid-1980s. Ralph won many trophies on the 3D competition archery range before focusing on deer and turkey hunting. His accomplishments include inventing the first of its kind tree climbing step system called "Fas-steps" - which were marketed by Warren & Sweat Tree Stands. His bowhunting stories have been published in numerous archery and bowhunting magazines. In 2009 he harvested the largest buck ever killed with bow and arrow in Columbia County, Georgia.

Ralph is retired from the US Army, and is presently a community college Professor of Business and Computer Information Systems.

"I'm always striving to be as good a man as my dog, Tuesday, thinks I am."
~ Ralph Blackwelder ~

Blackwelder
Books.com

Key to Good Reads

www.BlackwelderBooks.com

www.ingramcontent.com/pod-product-compliance
Lightning Source LLC
Chambersburg PA
CBHW051725090426
42738CB00010B/2086